everything

Chicago Public Library

Form 178 rev. 1-94

Wacky Wisdom

How to Do
Everything Unusual

Maurice Benziger

CRESCENT
BOOKS

Copyright © 1996 by Diagram Visual Information Ltd.
All rights reserved under International and Pan-American
Copyright Conventions.

No part of this book may be reproduced or transmitted in any form or by
any means electronic or mechanical including photocopying, recording,
or by any information storage and retrieval system, without permission
in writing from the publisher.

This 1996 edition is published by Crescent Books,
a division of Random House Value Publishing, Inc.,
40 Engelhard Avenue, Avenel, New Jersey 07001.

Crescent Books and colophon are registered trademarks of
Random House Value Publishing, Inc.

Random House
New York • Toronto • London • Sydney • Auckland

Printed and bound in the United States

A CIP catalog record for this book is available
from the Library of Congress.

Book design by Richard Oriolo

ISBN 0-517-14939-7

8 7 6 5 4 3 2 1

Contents

How to Improvise an Oil Lamp

Cut a slice off a cork. Pierce a hole in its center and thread a thin piece of cotton twine through it, leaving about 1 in to stick out at either side. Fill a glass about two-thirds full of water, then very slowly pour some cooking oil on top to make a layer about 1 in deep. Gently float the cork on the oil, allow a few moments for the wick to absorb the oil, and light it. If you haven't got any cotton twine, twist a dozen strands of sewing thread together to form a single, thick strand. Tie knots along its length to keep the threads in position; if you've more patience you can even braid them.

How to Make a Birch Bark Torch

You need a strip of very thick birch bark about six inches (15 cm) wide and two feet (60 cm) or so long. It may curl into a natural coil but if it doesn't, coil it and pull it into a tube and then tie with string at the outside end to keep it coiled. Before you tie the string, insert a stick into the opening at the other end, as a handle.

Simply light the end and hold the torch upright and it will give you light for about fifteen minutes. If the flame looks as if it is failing, wave it around for a moment or two. This kind of torch is not as reliable as a static illumination, since it needs the movement of being carried. Birch bark torches were used to light the trail by the Chippewa Indians of the Great Lakes area.

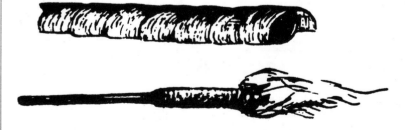

How to Keep a Campfire Lit

The papery bark of the silver birch will burn easily and keep your fire lit until larger branches become hot enough to catch fire.

How to Cook in the Earth

Dig a hole, line it with large stones, then light a fire inside it. Prepare your food and then, when you are ready to cook, scrape out most of the fire. Wrap pieces of meat and vegetables in banana leaves (or in burlap soaked in salad oil if you don't have banana leaves or their equivalent handy) and place on top of the hot stones and remaining ash. Pile the hot coals back on top and seal carefully with soil. There should not be any steam or smoke escaping. Leave for six or seven hours – it may take less time to cook but once opened the oven cannot be sealed again – and dig out your meal. Variations on this kind of oven are used in Papua, Hawaii, Madagascar, Mexico, and many other parts of the world.

How to Make a Camel Dung Cigarette Lighter

Find a small, lidded tin (the kind that some throat lozenges come in is ideal), a piece of flint, and a piece of ironstone. Fill your tin with dried camel dung, or horse dung, or any fibrous type of animal dung. Use the raised lid of the tin to provide shelter from the wind, strike the flint on the ironstone so that the sparks fall on the dung, blow gently – and you should have a glowing patch of dung from which to light your cigarette. This type of lighter was used by soldiers during the North African desert campaigns of World War II.

How to Make a Tripod

To prevent a hot plate from marking your table top, make an instant stand from readily available items. Put three forks, the backs of the prongs facing upward, through a napkin ring; spread the handles out so that they are equidistant, and you have a tripod on which to rest the plate.

How to Divine for Water

You need a divining rod. The traditional material is a forked stick of hazel, but other twigs have been used. Some dowsers (water diviners) prefer to use Y-shaped rods made of metal or whale bone. Hold the rod between the thumb and first finger of each hand, with the hands palm upward and elbows into the sides but not stiffly held. If you have the gift of "finding," the rod will either dip or rise when you are over a source of water. People also use divining rods for locating minerals. Some dowsers use a pendulum, a weight on a short length of string held between finger and thumb. When water is located, the pendulum starts to rotate or swing. Some dowsers claim to be able to locate water by holding a pendulum over a map. Scientists say there is no scientific explanation for water divining.

How to Distill Water

Distilled water is deionized water. To deionize the water, boil it and cool the steam: the condensed steam is distilled water. Alternatively scrape the ice from the sides of a freezer or the ice-making compartment of a refrigerator. When it melts, you've got distilled water.

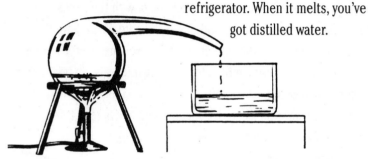

How to Make It Rain

If clouds pass overhead but do not release their moisture, you can fly through them in an airplane and release silver iodide smoke to "seed" them. This supercools and condenses water droplets in clouds, but is not always effective. Another method is to release water drops into clouds which collide and coalesce with the cloud's water droplets and so set off a rainfall pattern within the cloud. If no clouds appear you could try a rain dance. Throughout recorded time, attempts have been made to influence rainfall. The snake dance of the Hopi Indians of 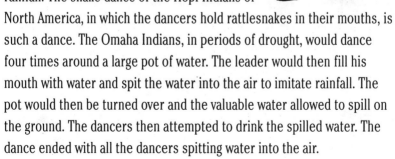 North America, in which the dancers hold rattlesnakes in their mouths, is such a dance. The Omaha Indians, in periods of drought, would dance four times around a large pot of water. The leader would then fill his mouth with water and spit the water into the air to imitate rainfall. The pot would then be turned over and the valuable water allowed to spill on the ground. The dancers then attempted to drink the spilled water. The dance ended with all the dancers spitting water into the air.

How to Track a Field Mouse

The field mouse's tiny tracks will probably only be visible in the snow. They consist of tiny footprints with the curved marks of the tail imprinted through the center of the tracks.

How to Track a Deer

Deer tracks can be recognized by their comma-like shapes. The size of the prints indicates the type of deer that made them.

How to Track a Raccoon

The tracks shown here indicate that a raccoon has recently used the path.

How to Throw a Lariat

It is pointless to try throwing a lariat made from unsuitable rope. You need good, strong rope, about 3/8-in thick, to provide the right degree of stiffness. The best length is about 35 ft.

A   B   C   D

Preparing the rope:

Form a loop about 4 in long (A, B). Pass the other end through the loop to form a noose about 4 ft long as it hangs, and hold it as shown (C). Coil the rest of the rope and transfer it to the left hand, with the strand that leads to the noose gripped between thumb and forefinger (D).

Throwing the lariat:

Practice throwing at a fence post about 10 ft away, and gradually increase the distance.

1 Stand holding the rope as shown.

2 Raise the right hand above the head, and begin to twirl the noose in a clockwise direction (as seen below). If the rope is not twisted, the noose should fill out into a circle.

3 Keep your eye on the target, and at the moment you throw the noose, step out with one foot. When you can rope the post consistently at 30 ft, you are good enough to be a cowboy.

How to Roast Chestnuts

The ideal way is to have a special chestnut roasting pan with a perforated bowl and long handle which you can hold over an open fire or stove, but you can also place them on the bars of a fire grate or in the embers of a campfire. If you want to cook them in the kitchen, shake them in a pan over the stove as if they were popcorn. For a slightly softer nut put them in a heat-proof dish with a little water and roast them in the oven for about 10 minutes.

Whatever method you choose, you must prepare them first, or they may explode and whizz around like bullets. This may sound fun but it leaves you with the contents all over the place and empty skins. Many people puncture the skin of the nut with a fork but a better way to make sure they do not explode is to cut a ring around the domed surface of each nut. And don't forget to salt them before you eat them!

How to Get Power from Potatoes

You will need:

    12 strips of zinc, 12 strips of brass, 24 paper clips, 12 potatoes, copper wire, 1.5 volt flashlight, bulb and holder.

    Cut your strips from sheets of scrap metal. Push one strip of each metal into each potato. Link the inserted brass strip to the inserted zinc strip with copper wire. Turn the wire a few times around each strip and hold in place with a paperclip. Complete the circuit by connecting the terminals of the bulb holder. Insert the bulb and it will light up.

How to Split a Log

Instead of trying to saw a log in half, make a slit in the top of the log with a saw and insert a metal wedge (A). Strike the wedge sharply several times with a mallet (B), and the log should split along the grain.

How to Tie a Bowline

First make an overhand loop in the main part of the rope (A). Bring the free end up through the loop, behind the main line, then down again through the loop (B); pull the knot tight. Use a bowline to tie a rope to a pole, or around your waist.

A   B

How to Tie a Clove Hitch

A clove hitch around a bar is made by looping the rope around and tucking it in as shown in the diagram above.

How to Make a Square Knot or Reef Knot

Put the two ends of the rope together and twist the first one over and under the second one as shown (A). Loop the second end above the knot, and twist the first end over it again (B). The knot is tightened by pulling both ends.

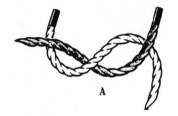

A

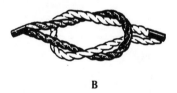

B

How to Climb a Rope

Begin by gripping the rope with both hands in front of your face and securing it between the sole of one foot and the top of the other (A). Climb by moving first your hand grip then your foot grip farther up the rope (B).

B

A

How to Build a Teepee

You need wood poles, a crescent shape of buffalo hide or bark fabric, and plenty of rope to make the traditional shelter of the Sioux Indians. A ceremonial teepee (or tipi) 20 ft (6 m) high and 30 ft (9 m) across requires about 50 buffalo skins, a small one only a few. All need three main poles plus lesser ones according to size. Sew hides or bark fabric together to form an open-topped cone, but sew only the top of the final seam, leaving about 7 ft (2 m) open for an entrance flap. Sew thongs to either side of this flap to tie it shut and attach a long rope to the edge of the cone. Lay three main poles on the ground, lay the cover over them, and raise the poles at the center. Flick the rope attached to the cover around the tops of the poles and pull it taut while the poles are adjusted into a stable position. Bring lighter poles under the cover, put their top ends through the center space to rest against the main poles, and their lower ends as far out as possible in an equidistant circle. These support the covering. Peg the bottom of the cover to the ground making use of pre-cut slits, or weight with stones. By careful juggling of the poles the wind can be prevented from blowing straight down the opening at the top. With a very large teepee the covering could be made in sections, laced together around the already erected holes and then hauled into position.

How to Make a Compass

Take an ordinary needle. Stroke it with one end of a magnet from the eye to the point, again and again. Always lift the magnet well clear of the needle at the end of each stroke. Cut a thin circle from a cork. Push the needle through the cork or glue or tape it to the top. Float the cork in a bowl of water. The needle will lie from north to south. If you stroke it with the south pole of the magnet, the point will point north, and vice versa.

How to Spot the Pole Star

Polaris, the Pole Star or North Star, is relatively easy to find in the night sky if you can first find Ursa Major, a constellation which is known by many local names: the Great Bear, the Big Dipper, or the Plough.

This constellation is, thankfully, quite easy to locate and looks a bit like a saucepan with a bent handle. The two stars on the right are known as the pointers. Imagine a line drawn through them and extend it for about five times the distance between the pointers and there is Polaris.

How to Calculate the Distance of a Thunderstorm

Sound and light travel at different speeds, which is convenient in measuring roughly how far away a thunderstorm is. A lightning flash may be seen at almost the moment it occurs since its light travels at approximately 186,000 miles (300,000 km) per second. Sound travels much more slowly, at about 760 mph (1223 kmph), so that by timing the difference between seeing the flash and hearing the peal of thunder, we can estimate how far away the storm is. One second difference is about a fifth of a mile or 340 meters away.

How to Tell the Direction of the Wind

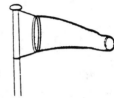

You can tell the direction of the wind by wetting a finger and holding it up – the windward side feels cold. A swiveling vane or weathercock will point to windward and a tube of fabric, narrow-

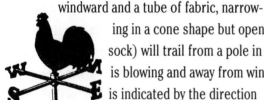

ing in a cone shape but open at both ends (a windsock) will trail from a pole in the direction the wind is blowing and away from windward. Wind direction is indicated by the direction from which it blows. The West wind blows from the west. The wind used always to be named by the compass points and their divisions, but in meteorology the direction is now given in degrees of a circle.

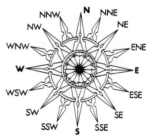

How to Describe the Strength of the Wind

The international scale used to describe the strength of winds was devised by Sir Francis Beaufort, a British admiral at the time of Nelson. It rates winds from calm to hurricane – "that which no canvas could withstand" as Beaufort originally put it. For official readings, measurements are taken at 32.8 ft (10 meters) above the ground, where speed will be considerably more than at ground level. When a meteorological report says that a wind is of Force 4, or Gale Force 9, it is the Beaufort Scale to which it refers.

Beaufort Scale	Character of wind	Beaufort Scale	Character of wind
0	calm	7	moderate gale
1	light air	8	fresh gale
2	slight breeze	9	strong gale
3	gentle breeze	10	whole gale
4	moderate breeze	11	storm
5	fresh breeze	12	hurricane
6	strong breeze		

How to Tell How Long Until the Sun Sets

Face the setting sun. Hold both arms at full length in front of you. Bend the fingers inward, parallel to the horizon, and fill the space between the horizon and the sun with your fingers. For each finger count 15 minutes, add that up and you'll know approximately how long it is until sunset. Of course, if you are in hilly country you will have to make allowance for the horizon not being the edge of the earth as it would be on a wide plain, but even making a guess with an imaginary horizon in woods and hills you'll still be fairly accurate – and it doesn't matter how tall or big your hands are either.

How to Tell the Time by the Sun

At noon the sun is due south of an observer in the northern hemisphere (due north of an observer in the southern hemisphere). So if you know the direction of due south you can also tell when it is noon. The change from night to day is caused by Earth turning upon its own axis, and so is the apparent movement of the sun across the sky from east to west. The spinning movement of Earth is regular and the sun appears to move through 15° every hour. So, knowing that the sun is due south at noon, and that the sun is moving through 15° every hour, enables us to be able to locate roughly where the sun will be at any given time – that is, when it's daylight!

How to Know What Clouds Bring

1 Cirrus are fine wispy clouds made from tiny spikelets of ice. They are sometimes called "mares' tails," and if more cloud follows then it is likely to rain.

2 Fine Weather Cumulus are small fluffy clouds, a little like those in children's drawings. If they are well spread out in a clear sky you can expect fine weather. But if before noon they form into rows, or "streets" as they are called, then you can expect the weather to deteriorate.

3 Cirrostratus are high-flying clouds frequently giving an almost complete overcast. Haloes around the sun usually mean that rain is on its way.

4 Altocumulus are long, flattish-looking clouds which frequently herald changeable weather.

5 Cumulonimbus have big "anvil heads" and often mean thunder, lightning, and sometimes hail. The upcurrents in these clouds are very powerful. Watch and you will see the clouds continually changing shape.

6 Cumulus are big bumpy looking clouds which often mean showery weather.

How to Improvise Water Wings

A temporary flotation aid can be improvised in an emergency from a pair of pants. If opportunity allows, the wings are more easily made on dry land, but you should practice taking your pants off while treading water.

1 Knot the end of each leg, and fasten the buttons or zip at the fly.

2 Hold the pants by the waistband behind your head.

3 Swing your arms quickly over and down into the water, so as to trap the maximum air inside.

4 Climb between the inflated pants as shown. Reinflate as necessary.

How to Get into a Life Preserver

Learn this one by heart before you need it, practicing in a shallow pool. The trick is harder than you'd think, and you won't have the book with you in the water!

1 Grip the near edge of the life preserver, with your hands on top.

2 Pull the ring close to your chin, then push downward.

3 As the ring reaches a vertical position, push the bottom edge away.

4 As the ring falls over your head, get your arms and shoulders through it.

How to Escape from Quicksand

As soon as you feel yourself sinking, throw yourself out flat to your full length and then very smoothly, with no further sudden movements, either swim or crawl back to where you walked in.

Don't give up until you get there.

Quicksand holes are often quite small, you are probably only inches from safe ground.

How to Recognize Gold

Gold stays bright forever: it does not tarnish or corrode when treated with normal chemicals. It is very soft and rarely used without the admixture of other metals, although as gold leaf it can be beaten very thin and so is not too expensive to use. It is assessed either in parts per thousand of pure gold or in carats (24 carats would be pure): 916 (22 carats), 750 (18 carats) and 375 (9 carats) are some of the proportions frequently used. In Britain 9 carats is the lowest grade permitted, in the US it is 10 carats and in many countries it is 14 carats. Ancient European and Asian gold usually contains small quantities of iridium which the Greeks and Romans could not remove (its absence is one way of recognizing fake gold antiquities). Precolumbian peoples used to mix their gold with copper to make an alloy called tumbago, a reddish gold. The easiest way of identifying gold is to look for a hallmark – but not all gold is hallmarked. Viewing under a spectroscope will give an accurate analysis of what you see but may fail to detect that the gold is only a thin surface plating. A third way is to take a tiny shaving and either subject it to tests with nitric and sulfuric acid or heat it until it melts and all the impurities disappear and only the gold remains. You can then measure the proportion of pure gold that is left.

How to Signal from Ground to Air

If you have to make a crash landing or bail out from an airplane, you will need to communicate with rescuers in the air. Here are some internationally recognized signals, which you can trample in snow or mark out with sticks or stones, cloth, or even parts of a wrecked plane. They are deliberately very simple shapes and need to be made on a large scale to be visible from the air.

L⌐	Aircraft badly damaged	LL	All is well
I	Serious injuries, need doctor	⋙	Send firearms and ammunition
II	Need medical supplies	:	Need signal lamp or radio
F	Need food and water	K	Show direction to proceed
△	Probably safe to land here	☐	Need map and compass
↑	Am proceeding in this direction	I>	Will attempt to take off
L	Need fuel and oil	W	Send engineer

How to Signal by Semaphore

Semaphore is a visual signaling system using the position of two hand-held flags to indicate the letters of the alphabet. To send a semaphore message the signaler holds the flags for a moment in the appropriate position for each letter in the message before switching them to the next letter.

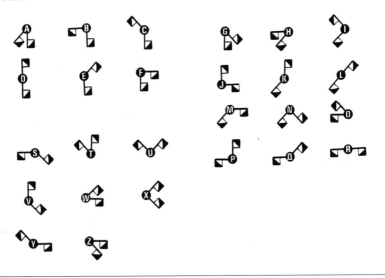

How to Decode Morse

Morse code enables messages to be sent, letter by letter, using a system of long and short signals, produced by depressing the key of an electric buzzer or any other continuous lone sound source, or by flashes of light from a flashlight, or even by puffs of smoke. Make a short pause between words to help the recipient. Dots in the key below represent short signals, dashes long ones.

The two best known messages to be sent by morse are probably the international distress signal SOS (. . . – – – . . .) and V for Victory (. . . –) beamed to occupied Europe by the Allies during World War II, or used musically to introduce broadcasts by them: it appears below as the opening notes of Beethoven's Fifth Symphony.

A .–	B –...	C –.–.	D –..	U ..–	V ...–	W .––	X –..–
E .	F ..–.	G ––.	H	Y –.––	Z ––..	1 .––––	2 ..–––
I ..	J .–––	K –.–	L .–..	3 ...––	4 ....–	5	6 –....
M ––	N –.	O –––	P .––.	7 ––...	8 –––..	9 ––––.	0 –––––
Q ––.–	R .–.	S ...	T –				

How to Recognize a Vampire

Don't wait to see the vampire's fangs appear. Vampires have no reflection – so look into a mirror.

How to Surrender

If you are close to your enemy, hold your hands above your head. At a distance, wave or fly a white flag. If you are flying your own colors – in a ship or a fort, for example – you should haul them down.

How to Avoid the Evil Eye

A very ancient belief, particularly strong in Mediterranean countries, attributes to some people the power to bring harm just by a look. To protect yourself from the malignant gaze, you can reflect the evil back upon the ill-wisher with the image of another eye. Paint it on your walls, as ancient Egyptians did, on the bows of your boat, as fishermen still do in many countries, or wear a glass eye amulet, like the blue ones popular among tourists to the Greek Cyclades. Those Greek eyes have blue irises, though blue beads, not necessarily made to look like eyes, will also give protection – hence all those blue faience beads on Egyptian mummies. Hang blue beads in your house, on your pets and livestock, and wear them on your body. Another effective amulet is the pattern of a hand – the Hand of Fatima, Muhammad's daughter, which you may paint around the doorway of your house. Again, a blue color strengthens its effect. A pair of horns set up on the roof also defy the evil eye, and to distract such unknown enemies you may make, or wear, the representation of a powerful or obscene gesture, the horned hand or "cornuta" gesture of Italy and Malta, or the "fig" sign in which the thumb is squeezed between the fingers.

How to Dress Crab and Lobster

Twist the limbs off the boiled shellfish, crack the claws open with a hammer, and extract the meat. A lobster needs to be split along its entire length with a knife. The white and brown meat of the crab should be kept separate. The only parts you can't eat are the stomach sacs, the gills, the dark intestinal vein which runs down the tail, and the "dead men's fingers" found between the legs on the underside. The greenish-looking liver in the lobster's head is delicious and so is the coral – that's the bright red roe of the female lobster.

Scrub out and polish the shells. Mix the brown crab meat with seasoning and breadcrumbs, then pile it back into the center of the shell with the finely-chopped white meat arranged artistically around it. Lobster looks best if the pieces of meat are kept as whole as possible. The dressed crustacean may be decorated with hard-boiled egg.

How to Pluck Poultry and Game

It is easiest to pluck a bird soon after it is killed. Start on the breast and underside. Grip the feathers by the handful, jerking them out, but not so violently that you tear the skin. You'll be surprised how many feathers there are — and small ones, in particular, will float away on the slightest breath of wind, so make sure that you are away from drafts and don't move about so rapidly that you create any. Have a large container next to you to put the feathers into as soon as they are plucked. After the underside is done, turn the bird and pluck its sides leaving the wings and thighs until last. With the wings, it will probably be necessary to pull the strong quills out one by one, holding the wing firmly in the other hand.

How to Make Muesli

To make this healthy breakfast cereal, mix together varying amounts of the following ingredients until you find a mixture that pleases you: dried oatmeal, bran, wheat or corn flakes, wheatgerm, brown sugar, raisins, dates, dried bananas, dried apple, chopped nuts, dried apricots.

How to Roast an Ox

You will need a huge open fireplace or a flat, clear, but sheltered area outdoors, away from trees and bushes that might catch fire. If outdoors, dig a trench the length of your ox and about two feet (60 cm) deep. Embed the upright members of your spit firmly beyond each end of the trench. If you have to improvise a spit, you will need firm uprights with bearings to carry the spit shaft, a sturdy spit-shaft to which a cogged disk is welded or bolted, and gearing to a smaller wheel which can be turned by an electric or gasoline motor. Have a handcrank on the end too, in case of breakdown, but hand-turning a 700-lb ox would demand several strong men working together. Gear the shaft to turn very, very slowly. If you can make your spit-shaft in two pieces so that one fits over the other it will make getting the ox in position easier.

Get a wood fire going about two hours before you intend to start cooking; when you are nearly ready, beat it down to red-hot embers and pile on charcoal to come just above ground level. Skewer the carcass with the spit-shaft as close to the backbone as possible and fix it in position. You may want to wire the outside of the carcass to prevent pieces from falling off. Hang a drip tray beneath it. An average-size beast of perhaps 600 lb (270 kg) will take about 18 hours to cook.

Keep the heat fierce to begin with to seal in the juices. If it starts cooking too slowly all the insides may begin to decompose before the process is completed. Do not worry if the outside gets charred, it's important that all the meat is cooked to avoid food poisoning. After a few hours you can open up the belly so that the middle can roast more quickly. Basting is not essential but will satisfy the onlookers' need to see

some culinary activity. Reflectors and wind barriers on at least three sides will help cut down heat loss.

Have plans for some sort of overhead shelter in case of rain – and some firebuckets in case anything goes wrong. There must be a continual watch to supervise the cooking and keep off marauding dogs and humans. As an alternative you could use anthracite coal for the fire: it gives a steady, fierce, glowing heat, but it hasn't the attractive smell of wood smoke. If roasting an ox seems too ambitious, (and if you've ever done it, it is unlikely that you will want to do it again!) try a baron of beef instead (6-7 hours cooking) or a whole pig (8-9 hours), both of which are much easier to spit.

How to Estimate Tea and Coffee for a Party

If you are offering tea or coffeee in large quantities you can calculate on getting 90 cupsful from 1 pound of coffee and about 100 cupsful from 1 pound of tea.

How to Make Jello Set Quickly

Do not use the full amount of hot water to dissolve the gelatin. Top up the full measure with cubes of ice and stir them well in. That will bring the temperature down rapidly and speed setting.

How to Peel Tomatoes

Place them in a pan of hot water for five
minutes. The skin will then lift off easily.

How to Tell Nutmeg from Mace

It's not easy, for they have a similar taste, but nutmeg is a hard nut kernel which is usually grated and mace is usually obtained as a powdered spice. Both grow in Grenada in the West Indies and once, during colonial times, the local governor received instructions from London recommending that the island concentrate on growing mace, since its sales were increasing whilst the nutmeg market was in decline. This gave the governor an insurmountable problem: for the nutmeg is the kernel and mace is the layer between the nutmeg and the outer casing of the fruit.

How to Peel Onions without Tears

Fill the kitchen sink or a bowl with water, submerge your hands, and peel the onions under water.

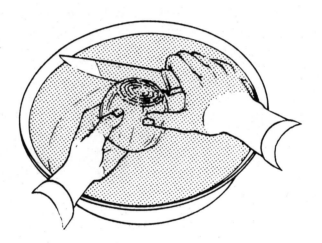

How to Stop Raisins from Sinking

Coating them in flour before using them will stop them from sinking to the bottom of cake batters.

How to Make Food Less Salty

Cook a whole, peeled potato with over-salty food; the potato will attract much of the salt and can be removed before serving. A little sugar will help disguise a salty taste.

How to Save on Lemons

If you want a drop or two of lemon juice, don't slice into a lemon. Pierce it with a skewer and squeeze out the drops you need. This way the whole lemon doesn't get dried out.

How to Crack a Coconut

Pierce the eyes with a large nail and drain out the milk. Put the coconut in the oven at a temperature of 325°F and leave it for a half hour. Let it cool. It may crack on its own – if it doesn't, tap it lightly with a hammer.

How to Personalize a Squash

Delight your friends and relatives by presenting them with a squash or similar vegetable bearing their names growing in the skin. The secret is to scratch the name lightly with any sharp-pointed instrument on the skin of the squash or other vegetable when it is first forming. The scar forms and grows as the squash grows and the name will be encrusted in large letters when it is fully grown.

How to Know Pasta by Its Shape

Italian noodles, spaghetti, and macaroni come in dozens of shapes and types. In northern Italy, the main types are flat ribbons (pasta bolognese), in the south they are tubular, made with eggs and dried so that they do not have to be used fresh. Some pasta is intended for baking, some for boiling, some for soup, and some to be stuffed.

FOR SOUPS

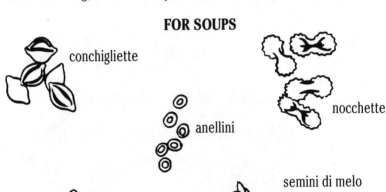

conchigliette

nocchette

anellini

semini di melo

acini di pepe

FOR BAKING

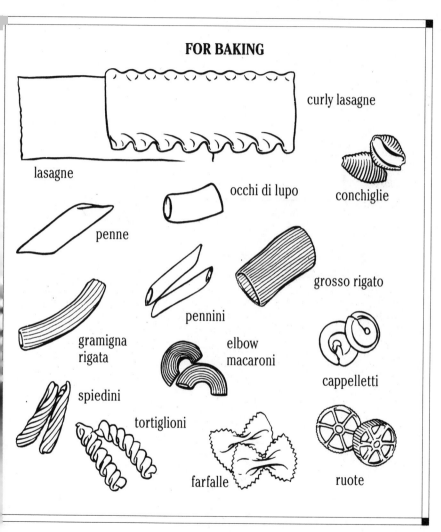

curly lasagne

lasagne

occhi di lupo

conchiglie

penne

grosso rigato

pennini

gramigna
rigata

elbow
macaroni

cappelletti

spiedini

tortiglioni

farfalle

ruote

FOR STUFFING

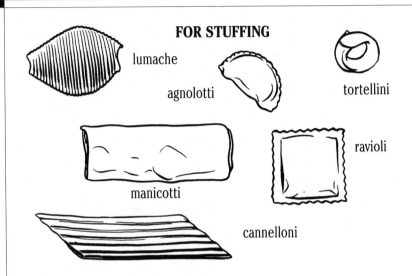

lumache

agnolotti

tortellini

manicotti

ravioli

cannelloni

FOR BOILING

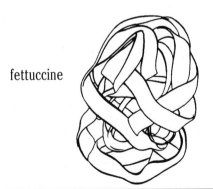

fettuccine

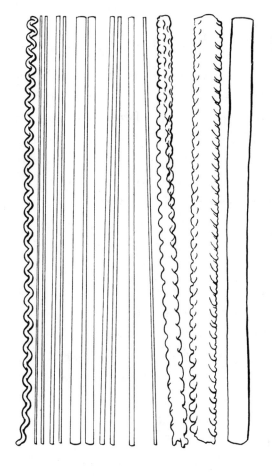

fuselli
capellini
fedelini
spaghetti
spaghettici
zite
mezzani
perciatelli
perciatelloni
lasagnette
linge di passeso
mafaldine
mafalde
zitoni

How to Use Chopsticks

Rest the thicker end of one stick in the saddle of the thumb (the flesh between the base of the thumb and the forefinger) and grip the lower part of that stick between the second and third fingers. Hold the other stick between the thumb and forefinger of the same hand, gripping it halfway or just above halfway along its length (the exact position will depend on what is comfortable for you), and articulate the tip of that stick against the lower one. If you have trouble getting the hang of it, use your other hand to shift the upper stick around until you get the right grip on it. When you can get the upper and lower sticks to pinch, you are ready to use them for picking up food. Part of the ritual of using chopsticks is to use a bowl instead of a plate for your food. Make a bed of rice onto which you can put other foods so their juices flavor the rice. Use small portions and add fresh rice as necessary. Hold the bowl as near your face as you feel etiquette permits or bend as near to the bowl as you wish to avoid spilling or dropping food. With foods more difficult to grasp, such as rice, you can use the sticks to shovel or flick them into your mouth. Remember: the principle is to keep the lower stick firmly in place and move the other stick against it.

How to Store Mushrooms

Mushrooms will keep fresh for longer if they are stored in a paper bag rather than a plastic one. The paper helps to absorb the moisture given out by the mushrooms.

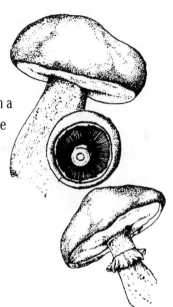

How to Hunt for Truffles

Find a pig with a sensitive sense of smell and make sure it has a ring in the end of its nose (otherwise it will snuffle up a truffle itself). Lead the pig around the trunk of trees growing in loamy soil, and when it starts showing interest in a patch, dig down carefully. If you are lucky, you will unearth one or more of the highly prized delicacies.

How to Dry Herbs

Herbs for drying should be gathered in the late morning on a fine day after the dew has dried from the plants. Some herbs should be dried on trays in a warm shady place such as in a linen closet, others should be hung in bunches in a dark place where it is dry, warm, and airy. If you want to keep the seeds, hang the bunch head-down in a paper bag.

Dry on trays	Dry in bunches	Difficult to dry
Bay	Mint	Balm
Basil	Sage	Borage
Camomile	Tarragon	Chervil
Parsley	Thyme	Chives
(dry quickly in a low oven)		Fennel
Marjoram		
Rosemary		

How to Store Cheese

Wrap cheese in plastic or a cloth and keep it in a cool place. Stored in the refrigerator, it needs to be taken out at least one hour before eating, or the cold lump will be tasteless. Hard cheese can be frozen, well wrapped in small packages, for up to eight months, but it needs to be at the right stage of ripeness before it is put in the freezer, and defrosted for 3-4 hours before eating. Potted cheese lasts a long time. Pound or crumble hard cheese and beat it with about one third of its weight of butter, a splash of white wine, and herbs or spices. Press it into a pot and pour some melted butter over it to keep out the air. You can pot blue-veined cheese like this, using red wine.

How to Make Yogurt

You need milk and a little store-bought live yogurt, one teaspoonful to two cups of milk. Bring the milk to a boil. For a creamier end-product, let it simmer for a half hour or longer to reduce. Pour it into a bowl and let it cool until it is just slightly warm. Mix the commercial yogurt with a little of the warm milk and stir the mixture into the bowl. Cover the bowl and leave it in a warm place for five to eight hours. Standing it in a pan of hot water set over the pilot light on a gas stove is ideal. You can use some of your newly-made yogurt to start off your next batch, and so on indefinitely.

How to Make Cottage Cheese

Put some freshly-made yogurt into a clean square of muslin laid across a strainer. Fold the corners of the muslin over the yogurt and leave it to drain overnight in a cool place. Next put the drained curds into a bowl, beat in some fresh cream, salt and any flavorings you like.

How to Make a Bouquet Garni

The basic bouquet used by French cooks consists of a sprig of parsley, a sprig of thyme, and a bay leaf. Tie them together and add them to dishes while they cook, removing them before serving. Some cooks prefer to take a piece of muslin and tie their herbs inside it. Just cut a 4 in square of cloth, place your herbs in the middle, pull the edges together, and tie a twist or two of thread around them. You can use dried herbs off the twig for this method. Individual cooks add their own herbs to the bouquet.

How to Open a Champagne Bottle

First make sure that the wine is well chilled, so it won't froth all over everything, and agitate it as little as possible. Champagne is a sparkling wine that builds up pressure within the bottle, which is why champagne bottles are extra thick and have their corks wired on. Twist the wire off the neck of the bottle, remove it and any foil or metal covering the cork. Keeping the bottle steady, gently ease the cork by pressure from the thumbs. Now grip the cork and twist it out very slowly. It should just pop out into the palm of your hand while a plume like a small puff of smoke rises from the bottle. Pour the champagne slowly into tall glasses to retain its effervescence. Of course, if you want to waste good wine you can serve it insufficiently chilled, shake the bottle, and push the cork out with your thumbs so that it makes an explosive noise, shoots across the room, and drenches everyone around in a fountain of champagne. Then pour it into glasses shaped like sundae dishes, mistakenly thought to be designed for champagne, which will allow it to go flat in no time!

How to Interpret Wine Labels

The information on wine labels varies from country to country. Basically, every label tells you the country of origin, the amount in the bottle, and the type of wine. Other information you may find includes the vintage, or year of production.

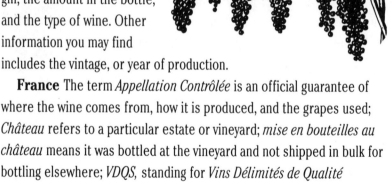

France The term *Appellation Contrôlée* is an official guarantee of where the wine comes from, how it is produced, and the grapes used; *Château* refers to a particular estate or vineyard; *mise en bouteilles au château* means it was bottled at the vineyard and not shipped in bulk for bottling elsewhere; *VDQS,* standing for *Vins Délimités de Qualité Supérieure,* is put on wines not up to Appellation standard; *Vins de Pays* are ordinary, local wines.

Germany The information on the labels is a guarantee of actual quality. The best wine is *QmP (Qualitätswein mit Prädikat)*; next comes *QbA*

(*Qualitätswein bestimmter Anbaugebiete*); below that is *Tafelwein,* dinner wine or everyday wine. The best wines carry the name of the vineyard (*Einzellage*) or group of vineyards (*Grosslage*). *Erzeugerabfüllung* means bottled by the grower. The variety of grape (generally *Riesling*) may also be named.

Italy The *DOC* (*Denominazione di Origine Controllata*) system is roughly equivalent to France's *Appellation Contrôlée.* The name of a wine may be the region where it is produced, a traditional name, or the kind of grape. *Classico* means the central part of the particular region.

Spain *Reserva* is a good quality wine; *Rioja* is the best wine region; a *Bodega* is a firm producing wines; *Denominacón de origen* is an "official" wine region.

United States Californian wines carry the brand name and the variety of grape used; similar information is found on labels from New York State.

England The name of the vineyard and the variety of grape used are the main information.

Australia Labels carry full details about the wines, but there are as yet no ''official'' standards of quality.

How to Taste Wine

If you're tasting wine before it's served to you in a restaurant, check the label and make sure the wine is what you ordered before the waiter draws the cork. A small quantity will be poured for you and you may be handed the cork. Some wine buffs believe they can tell everything about a wine by sniffing the cork. Then sniff the wine in the glass to get the aroma, and take a little on your tongue. If you like the flavor of this sip, then you'll enjoy the wine. There are no hard and fast rules, except that red wines should be at room temperature, while white and rosé (pink) wines should be cool. The sweeter the white wine, the cooler it can be. If the wine tastes of cork or is sour, don't accept it.

Professional wine tasters, who have a lot of different wines to try, don't actually swallow their mouthfuls, but spit them out. If they didn't, they'd soon be rolling drunk. They also like to eat a piece of cheese between tastes to cleanse the palate.

How to Make Anglo-Saxon Mead

Mead is a British alcoholic beverage known since the earliest times, drunk by the Saxons and right through the Middle Ages. This is a modern version of the recipe. You need:

4-5 lb (about 2kg) honey
2 oz (60 g) hops
the rind from 3-4 lemons
a small cloth bag

Sew the hops and the lemon rind into the bag. Add the honey to a gallon of water and boil it for an hour and a half; carefully remove the scum from the top. Add the bag and its contents. Allow to cool. When cold, place in a flask (preferably stoneware) and stopper it tightly. Allow to stand for 8-9 months before drinking.

How to Choose the Appropriate Glass

Glasses must be chosen both to be an appropriate size and to add to our enjoyment of what we are drinking. Long drinks need long glasses, so mixers served with ice are best in tall glasses, but spirits and wines need to be savored and their aroma held in glasses which have been evolved to match their character. Lagers, ales, and ciders are usually served in thicker glasses and many people claim they taste even better from silver tankards. Left to right, here are several types of glasses.

Champagne glass Shows the color of the wine and retains the bubbles. Champagne should not be served in shallow bowls like sundae dishes; they allow the bubbles to disperse too quickly.

Copita Traditional glass for sherry; funnels the scent. Half fill only.

White wine glass in style of Anjou. Slightly sloping sides concentrates bouquet; stem prevents hand from warming wine.

White wine glass in style of Alsace. Usually with a green stem which is reflected in the glass.

Cordial glass In addition to cordials, this 18th-century design is ideal for straight vodka and similar spirits. Fill to the brim.

Similar to the copita this glass is suitable for port, sherry, or madeira.

Hock glass The knobbed stem was fashioned to reflect its color into the wine.

Tulip glass Suitable for white or red wine and for champagne if no flute glasses are available. The in-turned rim helps to retain the bouquet.

Paris goblet Ideal for red wine. This fairly large glass should only be filled to about one-third.

Cognac glass It is easily cupped in the hand to warm the spirit and the vapor is retained in the bowl by the shape. Balloon glasses are not nearly so well matched to brandies.

Tall glasses are necessary if you have a long drink.

Thicker tumblers are suitable for beer. In Britain the thick glass "pub" tankard with a handle is traditional.

How to Mix the Perfect Martini

A martini – the cocktail, not the proprietary vermouth – consists of gin and vermouth in varying proportions according to taste, with a few other ingredients. It should be well stirred or, better still, shaken with cracked or crushed ice. If you do not have a shaker, a screwtop jar will serve the purpose.

RECIPES:

Extra dry: $1/7$ dry vermouth, $6/7$ dry gin, twist of lemon peel.

Dry: $1/5$ dry vermouth, $4/5$ dry gin, twist of lemon peel.

Standard: $1/3$ dry vermouth, $2/3$ dry gin, dash of orange bitters, twist of lemon peel, optional green olive.

Medium: $1/4$ dry vermouth, $1/4$ sweet vermouth, $1/2$ dry gin, twist of lemon peel, optional green olive.

Sweet: $1/3$ sweet vermouth, $2/3$ dry gin, dash of orange bitters, maraschino cherry.

Note: The olive or cherry should be impaled on a cocktail stick so that it can be removed while drinking.

How to Make Dandelion Wine

You need:

1 gal dandelion flowers
1 gal boiling water
3 lb sugar
orange peel
lemon peel
ginger root
yeast
piece of toast

Place the flowers in a large pan, pour boiling water over them, and stir well. Cover and leave standing for 3 days, stirring occasionally. Strain off liquid into pan, add sugar, peel, and ginger root (bruised). Boil for ½ hour, allow to cool, and add a little yeast on a piece of toast. Cover and leave to stand for 2 days, allowing yeast to work, then bottle. Leave bottles corked for several months before drinking.

How to Serve Beer

Lager beers, popular in the United States, Germany, and Scandinavia, are best served very cold. Most British and so called "heavy" beers, of which there are hundreds of varieties, are served at room temperature – chilling kills the flavor. To pour bottled or canned beer into a glass, tilt the glass and pour the beer against the side – that way you won't get too big a head on it. Don't shake the can or bottle beforehand. If you want a slight head, use a dry glass: a glass that's already been used tends to inhibit the froth. Generally, 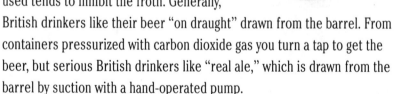 British drinkers like their beer "on draught" drawn from the barrel. From containers pressurized with carbon dioxide gas you turn a tap to get the beer, but serious British drinkers like "real ale," which is drawn from the barrel by suction with a hand-operated pump.

How to Make Granita

To make one quart (one liter) you need:

2 cups sugar

1 cup water

1 cup lemon juice (or other fruit juice)

1 cup ice and water

1 tbsp finely grated lemon rind (or other rind if appropriate)

Method

Dissolve the sugar in the water, heating it in a pan to make sure it dissolves completely and easily. Cool. Add lemon juice, rind, and ice and water. Stir until the ice is melted. Pour into freezer trays and freeze. When almost completely solid, take from the freezer and break up the mixture. You can use an electric beater to mix it if you run it on very slow, or mix by hand. Return to the freezer for an hour. Take it out and beat or mix again. Freeze again for one hour or until firm. Serve immediately as a dessert or even to accompany meat or salad.

An instant granita Put some crushed ice in a glass, pour milkshake syrup over it and a dash of cream. The syrup flavors the ice as it trickles through it.

How to Make Greek or Turkish Coffee

The people of the eastern Mediterranean like their coffee very strong and drink small quantities at a time from small cups. Choose a fairly strong coffee, medium roast, and finely grind or pulverize it. Place it in a copper coffee pot (you can make do with an ordinary small saucepan if the proper equipment is not available); about two tablespoons will do. Add four tablespoons of sugar. Mix, then add two cups of water. Heat until it rises in a froth. Remove from heat. Repeat twice. Add a little cold water and pour out gently. Some of the muddy lees will go into the cup but don't worry, that's expected; one never drinks it to the bottom! What you have made is what the Greeks call *glykí vrastos*, sweet and well boiled. If you want very sweet coffee, *poli glykós*, add more sugar. Medium-sweet coffee, known as *métrios*, a little sugar, *me olighi*, no sugar, *skétos*. Because you can boil up small quantities very quickly you can make each cup separately to please the tastes of each of your guests. Sip it slowly and, to increase your enjoyment, serve it with *loukoumi* (Turkish delight).

How to Blow a Cork into a Bottle

Lay a bottle on its side and in its mouth place a cork of slightly smaller diameter than the neck. Can you blow the cork into the bottle? Get your friends to try. If they blow into the bottle they will increase the pressure of air within and force the cork out rather than in. The method is simple enough if you know the trick: the secret is to suck air out, so that the pressure is reduced and the cork drawn in. You can produce the same effect by heating the bottle, so that some of the expanded air is expelled; as it cools again the air will contract, sucking in the cork.

How to Slice a Banana Before Peeling It

Insert a long needle into the flesh of the banana through the skin, and move it as far as possible from side to side. Do this at regular intervals along the banana, and when it is peeled, the flesh will be in neat slices.

How to Break a Thread in a Sealed Bottle

Take an empty wine bottle, screw a small hook into the base of the cork, and tie to it a thin thread with a small weight attached to the other end. Drop weight and thread into the bottle, insert the cork, and seal with sealing wax or tape. Now challenge your friends to snap the thread without breaking the seal or shaking the bottle. The way to do this is very simple, but not many people will guess how without being told. You can break the thread without even touching the bottle. Take it out into the sunlight and use a magnifying glass to concentrate the sun's rays until the thread burns through. Of course, you'll look pretty silly if you try this trick on a cloudy day!

How to Stand an Egg on Its End

Shake the egg vigorously to mix up the yolk and the white. Hold the egg upright for several minutes so that the heavier yolk sinks to the bottom. With a little patience, you will then be able to stand the egg on its broad end.

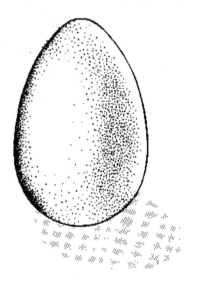

How to Make an Egg Swim

With a good supply of salt you can make an egg float halfway up a jar of water as if by magic. Fill one jar with plain water; the egg will sink (**1**). Fill another with a very strong solution of salt dissolved in water; the egg will float (**2**) because it is less dense than the solution. Fill a third jar with roughly equal quantities of the two liquids, and the egg will be suspended when the density of the solution matches the density of the egg (**3**).

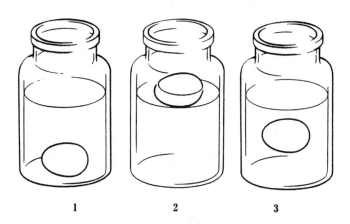

1   2   3

How to Tie a Knot While Holding Both Ends of a Piece of String

Take a piece of string at least 20 inches long. Challenge your friends to hold one end in each hand and to tie a knot without letting go of either end.

It's easy: fold your arms before you take hold of the twine. As you unfold them the knot will tie itself. You can use a scarf or a large handkerchief, held corner to corner, if you don't have any string.

How to Measure Your Head for a Wig

Five measurements should be supplied to order a wig:

1 Circumference of head: across forehead, behind ears, and around back of neck.

2 Forehead to nape of neck over top of head.

3 Ear to ear across forehead.

4 Ear to ear over top of head.

5 Temple to temple around back of head (horizontally).

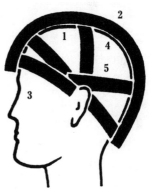

How to Read Your Palm

Does your hand reveal your character and your future? The more prominent a line or feature, the stronger the aspect it represents will be in your life.

1 Girdle of Venus: usually indicates bad character, too influenced by carnality.

2 Line of heart: affection and devotion.

3 Mount of Jupiter: ambition and pride.

4 Will and decision.

5 Logical power.

6 Line of Mars: warlike disposition.

7 Mount of Venus: love, melody, passion.

8 Line of life.

9 Bracelets of Life: each represents 30 years.

10 Mount of saturn: fatality.

11 Line of Fortune.

12 Mount of Apollo: riches or art.

13 Line of brilliance: success in art.

14 Mount of Mercury: wit, science.

15 Line of Health.

16 Mount of Mars: courage.

17 Line of head: reason.

18 Via Lascivia: faithlessness and cunning.

19 Mount of the Moon: folly or imagination.

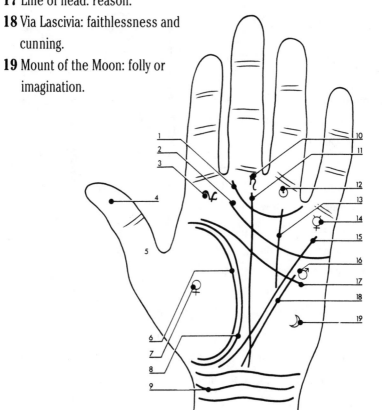

How to Measure Your Own Body

Equip yourself with a measuring tape – a real measuring tape, not a metal one that won't be flexible enough to go closely around your body – and paper and pencil to record your findings. One method is to stand against a wall and mark positions against it which you can then measure flat. It is not easy to do this accurately, but it is the only practical way of measuring your own height. If you stand opposite a

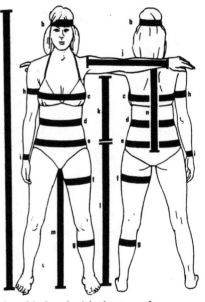

mirror you will be able to see if your hand is level with the top of your head. Hold a book or other flat surface on top of your head. Keep it in position while you turn and make your mark on the wall. Stay in front of the mirror to take horizontal measures too, then you will be able to make sure the tape is level and that it is not twisted. To measure your head, chest, waist, or hips settle the tape around you and then draw it against you with the end of the tape (which is frequently reinforced with a small piece of metal) overlapping the free end. Grip the point of overlap on the free end with your thumb exactly on that point. Keep hold as you release the tape and read off the measure at that point. Measure your chest both relaxed and expanded, and if you measure with your stomach pulled in be honest and measure it relaxed as well! Thighs and calves are easy; just wrap the tape around them. Wrists and arms are more difficult because you have to manipulate the tape with one hand. Shoulder to wrist: you'll need to hold the tape end at the shoulder and the other end between the fingers while contriving to keep the tape running along your elbow. Grip the tape between your fingers and pull it tight toward the shoulder until the top end is in place. Then with a little contortion you should be able to read off the measure at your wrist for both the bent and straight arm. From armpit to waist or thigh hold the end in your armpit and use the other hand to grip the lower point. For outside leg length, stand on the tape and draw it up under your foot until the end is at your waist Keeping your foot firmly on the tape, bend your knees and read the measure. Do the inside leg in the same way. Measurements down the back: hold the end at your neck, let the tape hang against your body, and then use the other hand to grip the point at which you need the measurement.

How to Find
Your Blind Spot

Hold this page at arm's length. Close or cover your left eye. Now look at the cross with your right eye. Slowly move the book toward you. At one point, the dot will disappear. Now look at the dot with your left eye in the same way. You will find that the cross will now disappear.

How to Take a Pulse

The easiest place to take a pulse is at the wrist, whether it's your own or someone else's. The fingers – not the thumb because the ball of the thumb has too strong a pulse of its own – should be lightly but firmly pressed over the radial artery. You'll find it about 1/3 inch (1 cm) from the thumb side of the wrist. Move your fingers around a little if you can't find it right away; you will feel the gentle throbbing. Count the number of beats in 30 seconds, using a watch with a second hand to make sure you time it exactly, then multiply by two. A healthy pulse can be very variable. The average resting adult's rate is 72 per minute but can range from 60-80; children have a higher rate and a baby's may be 140. If active or excited the pulse rate will increase. In cases of accident and loss of blood, especially suspected internal bleeding, take the pulse every five minutes, making a note of time and rate. A rising rate is an indication of continuing loss of blood.

How to Bandage a Finger

Cover the wound with sterile gauze and then a strip of narrow bandage (**1**). Wind the bandage around the finger toward the tip and down again (**2**), split the end (**3**), and tie around the base (**4**). A finger stock (**5**) helps keep the bandage clean and secure.

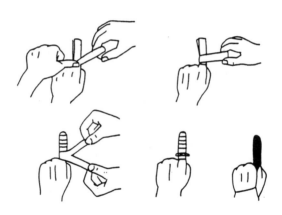

How to Cure a Hangover

At its simplest, a hangover is a reaction to dehydration: that headache means your brain's environment has been dried out by alcohol, the alcohol that the night before was popping brain cells and giving you that light-headed feeling. To counteract it, take in liquid: water or fruit juice, though fruit juice may upset the stomach. One school of thought recommends milk, which has the virtue of also coating and calming a stomach lining temporarily inflamed by alcohol. Coffee gives your brain the extra kick of caffeine; tea will do the same. Analgesic will relieve the pain, but the water you drink with it does more good for your eventual recovery by replacing badly needed fluid.

"Hair of the dog" – having a quick shot of whatever it was you were on last night works temporarily because of the liquid content of even the strongest drinks as well as the euphoria initially induced by the alcohol, but you are increasing the dehydration when the alcohol gets into your system so it's a bad idea and no cure for a hangover. If you've been drinking heavily, take a large glass of water before you go to bed to help to reduce the strength of the hangover when you wake up in the morning.

How to Make a Sling

A sling is used to protect and support an injured arm. The professional way of making one is to use a triangular bandage, though a square of cloth folded along the diagonal will do. You also need a safety pin.

Basic Method

A1 Place the arm across the body with the hand a little higher than the elbow. Put the open triangle cloth between the body and the arm with one corner stretching beyond the elbow. Another corner goes around the neck.

A2 Bring the third corner up and tie in front of the hollow above the collar bone. Fold the elbow corner forward and secure it with the safety pin.

For a more raised position If a more raised position is required, as in the case of an injured hand, fractured ribs, or if the patient needs extra support for a rough journey:

B1 Place the triangle over the arm, one corner well beyond the elbow. Ease the edge of the bandage between the arm and the body, cupping hand and arm, and carry the free end behind the body.

B2 Adjust to the required position and tie at the shoulder. Tuck the loose corner between the arm and the front part of the bandage and secure with the safety pin.

Improvised slings

Here are three ways to improvise a sling if no bandage or cloth is available.

C Place the hand and arm inside a buttoned jacket.

D Pin the sleeve containing the injured arm to the clothing.

E Make a supporting loop with a scarf, belt, or tie and suspend around the neck.

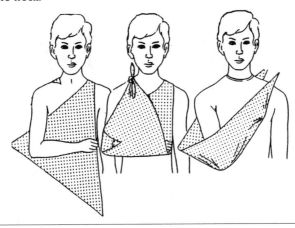

How to Cure Insect Stings

Bee and wasp stings are equally annoying, but require opposite treatments. Bee stings are acid and require an alkali to neutralize them; wasp stings are alkali and require an acid. Ammonia and vinegar are readily available remedies; an easy way to remember which is for which is that a and b (for ammonia and bee) are next to each other in the alphabet, and so are v and w (for vinegar and wasp).

How to Remove Bags Under the Eyes

A temporary method for removing bags under the eyes is to smear uncooked egg white over the affected skin. As it dries, the skin will tighten, but the effect only lasts an hour or two.

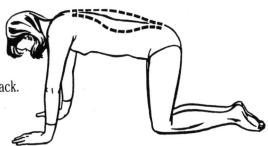

How to Ease a Backache

Kneeling on all fours and alternately rounding and hollowing your back is an excellent way of relieving the aches in your lower back.

How to Get to Sleep Without Pills

The traditional method is to count sheep – but for it to work you should make an effort to visualize each sheep jumping over a fence before you count it. Try closing your eyes and breathe regularly. As you breathe out, visualize your breath forming a cloud in front of you, as it does on a cold day.

Take deep breaths, hold the breath, and then exhale, counting each breath as you breathe out. In many people this produces a mildly hypnotic state.

Read a book– but not one with a gripping story or you will find you stay awake even longer!

Listen to the radio at low level

(using a time switch to turn it off after you have gone to sleep). Or do mental arithmetic – if you have a digital clock try to factorize the number on the clock screen – though that kind of mental stimulus may keep some people awake. Presumably it works by crowding other more disturbing thoughts from your surface consciousness.

As an aid to sleep, avoid heavy meals shortly before bedtime, or drinks containing caffeine (tea, coffee, and cola). Ensure that the mattress is firm and supports your body and that you are neither too hot nor too cold. And attend to nature's needs before retiring – a desire to empty the bladder or bowels is a common cause of sleeplessness.

How to Take Nasty Medicine

Terrible taste? Forget about trying to mix it with something nice. Eat a very strong peppermint immediately before taking it or suck an ice cube.

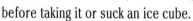

They will cause such a strong reaction in the taste buds that they won't even register the medicine as you gulp it down.

How to Ease a Toothache with Acupressure

Acupressure is a treatment of ailments by the pressure of the fingertips or fingernails at specific parts of the body. Pressure should be firm with a slightly rotary or boring movement applied at the same time. A treatment of from half a minute to four minutes is usually sufficient to bring results. A toothache can be treated by pressure on the point known as *Chang-lang*, at the root of the nail of the first (index) finger, close to the thumb-side corner, or at the *Kroun-Loun* point between the outer ankle and the Achilles tendon, with the pressure applied down onto the heel bone.

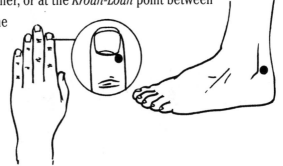

How to Do the Lotus

This is an advanced yoga position and many people will find it impossible at first. Go easy!

1 Sit on the floor and place the left foot as high up the right thigh as possible.

2 Bring the right foot into a similar position, crossing it over the lower left leg.

3 Form an "O" with the forefinger and thumb of each hand, and rest the fingers on each knee. Hold the posture as long as is comfortable.

How to Look Fat or Thin

A perfectly ordinary looking person can be made to look fatter or thinner with carefully applied stage make-up. Basically, you will need one tube of dark make-up and one of light or white. Cover your face with foundation before you start. For a lean face, put dark make-up in the hollows of the cheeks, the lines from nose to mouth, and the hollows in front of the temples (a); add pale highlights to the cheekbones, the top of the nose and the brows (b). For a fat face, put a rosy glow of the dark make-up on the cheeks, the chin, the tip of the nose and the forehead (c) and then highlight these with circles of white; wear cotton pads inside the cheeks to complete the illusion (d).

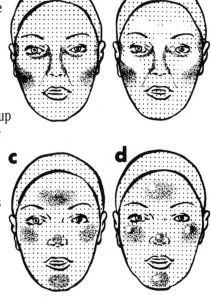

How to Increase Your Lifting Power

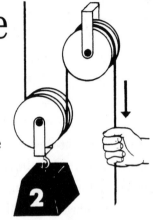

However strong you are there is a limit to the weight you can lift unaided – but over 2200 years ago the Greek mathematician Archimedes worked out a simple system.

By using two pulleys he could raise double the weight, by using four, four times as much, and so on. He demonstrated the method, with his own strength alone, by pulling a ship back into the sea which it had taken many men much effort to haul onto dry land.

A pulley is a variation on the principle of the lever and requires a firm place to which the pulley, or pulleys, can be attached. Each pulley is a pivoted disk around the edge of which runs a groove in which a rope or cable can run with minimum friction. In practice, blocks of pulleys are used to dispense with separate fittings and to simplify rope runs. These then require a matching pulley block at the point of attachment to the object to be lifted or hauled.

How to Make the Moutza Sign

This Greek insult can be made in five different strengths: all mean "go to the devil." Bring the arm forward toward the victim with the thumb and last two fingers folded and the first two in a V-sign. Make the same movement with the palm flat and all fingers spread (= x2). Do it with both hands at once (= x4). Push the sole of your foot at the victim as well (= x6). Push both feet forward and both hands (= x8). This is a very serious insult. Be careful not to raise your palm when politely refusing another drink or other offers in Greece; it is easily confused with the moutza sign.

1   2   3   4   5

How to Improve Your Memory

Eat chervil. According to one ancient source, this will prod the memory of old people.

How to Do the Cobra

The cobra is a yoga position designed to exercise the chest, arms, buttocks, and back.

1 Lie down on your front, forehead on the floor, hands palm downward beneath the shoulders.

2 Very slowly raise the head and push down with the hands.

3 Still moving slowly, arch the spine as far as possible without hurting, and hold this position for a few moments.

4 Lower yourself to position **1**, then relax, hands by the sides, and head turned to one side. Repeat the whole sequence.

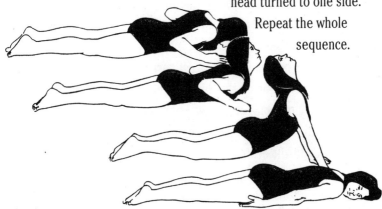

How to Bow Japanese Style

Japanese people bow to each other on numerous occasions: at first meetings, when making requests, when expressing gratitude, when saying goodbye. The Japanese bow is an act of self-abasement and humility, and it is probably this more than any peculiarly Japanese body structure 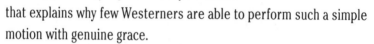 that explains why few Westerners are able to perform such a simple motion with genuine grace.

The proper bow begins from an erect posture, arms at the side, palms turned inward and resting on the thighs. Bend forward at the waist with a snappy, deliberate motion – not a sag. For a second or two, keep your body locked in the bow, eyes down, then return to the vertical. A bow with your upper body 10-20° off the vertical is sufficient for most situations. A bow of 30° is good for making an apology or requesting money. Anything more than that and you are either showing off or in such a bad spot that no amount of groveling can help you.

How to Use Neapolitan Sign Language

The people of Naples seem to talk more with their hands than they do with their tongue. This is not just to add emphasis to what they are saying; for centuries Neapolitans have used gestures with very exact meanings. Here are some of them from a book published a century and a half ago but still in use today. **1** Be silent **2** No **3** Beauty **4** Hunger **5** Derision **6** Fatigue **7** Stupidity **8** Beware **9** Dishonest **10** Crafty

Some, such as **1** and **5**, will be understood in many places, but **2** and **8**, although used elsewhere, may have very different meanings. In France, for instance, **8**, instead of meaning "watch out, danger," means "I'm watching you, don't go too far." Farther north in Italy and in France, **2** becomes very impolite and means "get lost" — or something stronger.

How to Talk to a Deaf Person

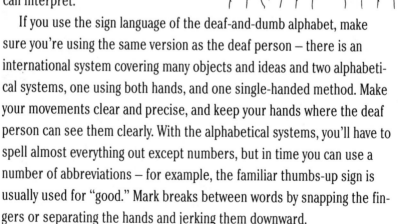

Most deaf people learn to lip-read, so always face a deaf person when you are speaking. Make sure you enunciate your words clearly and don't mumble – then your lips and tongue make easily visible movements that a deaf person can interpret.

If you use the sign language of the deaf-and-dumb alphabet, make sure you're using the same version as the deaf person – there is an international system covering many objects and ideas and two alphabetical systems, one using both hands, and one single-handed method. Make your movements clear and precise, and keep your hands where the deaf person can see them clearly. With the alphabetical systems, you'll have to spell almost everything out except numbers, but in time you can use a number of abbreviations – for example, the familiar thumbs-up sign is usually used for "good." Mark breaks between words by snapping the fingers or separating the hands and jerking them downward.

How to Follow the Language of the Fan

Fan language, much used by fashionable ladies in the 18th century, was of help in carrying out love affairs under the chaperone's watchful eye.

Here are some of the more useful signals:

With the fan open

I love you: hide the eyes behind the fan

I do not love you: give quick brushing away movements, holding the fan pointing downward, the back of the hand on top

You are welcome: hold the fan palm uppermost and extend toward the other person

I must avoid you: hold the fan over the head

With the fan closed and holding its tip to the face

Yes: touch the right cheek

No: touch the left cheek

Hush: touch the lips

Do not give us away: touch the left ear

I love you: point toward the heart

Go away you are boring me: yawn behind the fan

How to Handle a Tarantula

Despite its reputation, a tarantula spider is generally no more dangerous than a wasp or a bee. It is best kept in a covered container in case it escapes and frightens people; an aquarium tank with air holes is ideal. A dish of water with a sponge on it will be needed for it to brush its mouth against for moisture; spiders do not drink in the way we do. You can also spray a fine mist of water onto the sides of the tank. Feed it insects or even small mice. If you have problems with cockroaches or other insects and pests, you could let your spider out on a leash. (One spider enthusiast cleared his apartment of cockroaches in a matter of days.)

Just in case you are one of those rare people for whom a tarantula bite could be very dangerous, avoid touching it. Handle it carefully, with tongs if necessary.

How to Attract Butterflies

You can do this by growing aubretia, honesty (silver dollars), petunias, lavender, buddleia (butterfly bush), michaelmas daisies, and cabbages in your garden.

How to Trap Slugs

Sink a saucer full of beer level with the surface of the garden soil. Slugs will be attracted to the beer and become trapped in the saucer. With luck, toads or birds will come and eat them for you.

How to Catch a Cockroach

Switch off the light at night so that the cockroaches are tempted to emerge, and have a bar of soap ready.

Switch the light on suddenly, and pounce on the cockroaches as they scurry for safety. Trap them by pressing the bar of soap over them.

How to Ride an Ostrich

Climb on the middle of the bird's back, seat yourself as far to the rear as possible, while still able to keep your seat, and grip the roots of its wings. Then hang on. The ostrich will probably run in the hope of shaking you off.

They are large and tough birds. In South Africa, where ostriches are farmed, an ostrich race is often part of rural festivities. If they go in for it in a big way, ostrich jockeys tend to wear jockey outfits like those worn for horse racing, but ostrich racing is a rather undisciplined, ad hoc event. Ostriches are curious and friendly but they are independent spirits and not really trainable for organized events.

How to Teach a Parrot to Talk

The African gray parrot and the Amazon parrots of South America are among the best mimics of the bird world. Individuals vary in their ability to learn and a great deal depends on the perseverance of their teacher. The higher register of a woman's or child's voice is believed to be easier for most birds to copy. Patient repetition in a darkened room without distractions is the key to success. To avoid losing too much of your own time, record the phrase you wish the bird to copy on a loop tape, and play it for ten minutes a day. Birds also learn to associate words. A telephone ringing may prompt a parrot to say "Hello" and repeat the number, or a faucet turned on may be a cure for the bird to make the sound of running water. Attempts to mimic something may at first be very garbled but they become clearer with practice.

How to Make a Cake for Birds

Fill a small basin with any mixture of millet, birdseed, chopped bacon rind, shelled peanuts, and coconut, and add enough suet to make the mixture pliable. Press it down hard into the basin, chill, and when it is firm turn the cake out; put it on a cat-proof bird table.

How to Attract Birds

In the summer Birds feed themselves, but they like somewhere to drink and bathe. To give them sanctuary, make a shallow stone or cement birdbath, no more than two inches deep, with a rough edge and bottom so that the birds can get a footing. Put it on the top of a pillar or post that cats can't climb.

In the winter Birds appreciate help with finding food. Make a bird feeder, on a cat-proof post. Ideally, it should have two platforms, one open, the other enclosed with 11/2-inch mesh wire netting to let in small birds and keep the bigger bullies out. For food, put out grains such as rice (boiled or raw), bread, seeds, scraps of meat or bacon, and a lump of hot cereal which they can peck at and which won't freeze. Chickadees and other titmice will appreciate nuts, hung in a wire cage to which they can cling and other birds can't.

116

How to Get Carp to Come When You Call

Call your goldfish to the pond edge by ringing a handbell or banging the side of the pond with your palm. These sounds will create stronger vibrations in the water than your voice will. Then drop flake or pellet fish food into the water in one area only. Do this every day at feeding time, always making the same noise and dropping food in the same area. Soon you will find the fish will respond to the signal without waiting for the food to be dropped in the water. Lengthen the time between calling and feeding them and you will have fish coming asking to be fed. They may even come in response to your footsteps as you approach the pond. In the same way, if you have a largish indoor aquarium, you will probably be able to train fish to come to one side of the aquarium when you tap on the glass.

How to Please a Piranha

Feed it meat and keep it in running or constantly circulating water at about 77°F, for it comes from the warm rivers of South America. It prefers its food live and, since it can grow to 9 in long, keep your fingers out of the water because it may bite the tip of one of them. Watch these carnivores in action and you won't take any risks.

How to Hold a Goldfish.

Holding a fish can remove the mucus that coats its body and protects its skin from organisms in the water, but sometimes it may be necessary when inspecting or treating for disease. First, put your hand in the water with the fish until it cools down to the fish's temperature. Fish do not easily tolerate sudden  changes in temperature. Whether taking a fish from the water or lifting it from a net, allow the fish to swim or slide into your lightly cupped hand between thumb and index finger. Then close your hands around it. The fish must be gripped firmly so it cannot wriggle and damage itself, and its fins must lie naturally against the body.

Whenever possible transfer fish in a net or even a spoon or ladle.

How to Race a Crocodile

Don't fool yourself: if you are ever chased by a crocodile remember that it can run very fast indeed! But, fortunately a crocodile cannot make sudden changes in direction. To outwit your pursuer, don't run straight, make a series of zigzags: but make it snappy. If you don't, the crocodile will.

How to Tell a Frog from a Toad

The differences between frogs and toad are best observed by comparing an example of each. If this is not possible, the texture of the skin is the easiest characteristic to assess.

	FROG	**TOAD**
skin	smooth & damp	drier, warty
head	long & narrow	short & broad
body	slim, waisted	short, squat
hindlegs	usually long	shorter
movement	hops	hops, walks, runs
spawn	clustered	in ribbons

How to Measure a Horse

The size of a horse is given by its height at the withers, the highest point on its back at the base of its neck. It is expressed in "hands" – a unit based on the width of a human hand – in practice considered to be a measure of 4 in. The height is given to the nearest inch so that a pony measuring 50 inches is said to measure 12.2 hands (12 hands plus 2 inches).

How to Name the Points of a Horse

The features of a horse's anatomy, or its points, have special names. Here are the main ones:

1 Forelock **2** Muzzle **3** Windpipe **4** Elbow **5** Forearm **6** Knee **7**Cannon **8** Fetlock joint **9** Hoof **10** Pastern **11** Chestnut **12** Flank **13** Stifle **14** Shannon **15** Hock **16** Gaskin **17** Tail **18** Thigh **19** Dock **20** Croup **21** Loins **22** Back **23** Withers **24** Shoulder **25** Crest **26** Mane **27** Poll

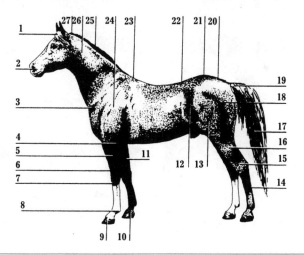

How to Name a Horse's Gait

A horse has four natural gaits: the walk, with speed of about 4 mph, (about that of the average person); the trot, 9 mph; the canter, 10-12 mph; and the gallop for even faster speeds.

1 The walk: The horse raises one foot after the other and puts them down in the same order.

2 The trot: The front leg on one side of the body strikes the ground at

the same time as the hind leg on the other side.

3 The canter: This involves three beats: first one forefoot hits the ground, then the other forefoot and the opposite hind leg, then the other hind foot.

4 The gallop: The hind legs are bought forward together and the horse proceeds in leaps, stretching out its forelimb. Sometimes all hooves are off the ground at the same time.

How to Offer Food to a Horse, Donkey, or Camel

All may be fed by fitting a nose bag over the animal's head or by placing the food in a manger at a convenient height. If you offer tidbits from your hand, hold your hand absolutely flat with the food lying on top – or you may find it is your fingers that get eaten.

How to Get an Old Cat to Accept a New Kitten

Make the kitten smell like the established cat before they meet. If your cat uses a litter tray, rub the kitten with some soiled litter, or rub it with a blanket from the cat's basket or a cushion that the old cat sleeps on, which will be impregnated with its smell. The older cat will then feel that the kitten is part of his or her property and will, if you are lucky, start to wash it.

How to Medicate a Cat

If your cat becomes ill it may be necessary to medicate it at home. Here are instructions to make it as trouble free as possible. Two people may be needed; one to hold the cat, the other to give the cat the medicine. To prevent scratching, restrain the cat as shown (a) or by wrapping in a towel. Place pills at the back of the cat's throat (b) and stroke the throat to encourage swallowing. Pour liquid medicine into the side of the cat's mouth from a dropper (c). Hold the cat's mouth shut until the medicine has been swallowed.

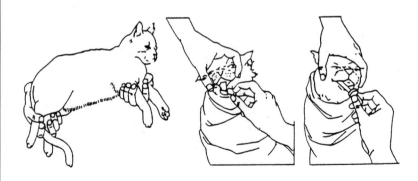

How to Teach a Dog to Beg

Sit your dog in the corner of a room where the angle of the walls will help it to balance. Giving the command "beg," lift the dog's foreleg up to its chest with the one hand while holding a tidbit above its head with the other. Practice until you can take your supporting hand away. Almost all adult dogs can be taught how to beg, but greedy ones learn the fastest. Do not try to teach a puppy, as its back muscles will not be strong enough to hold the pose. Wait until it is 9 months to a year old.

How to Name the Points of a Dog

As with the horse, the "points" or anatomical features of the dog have special names.

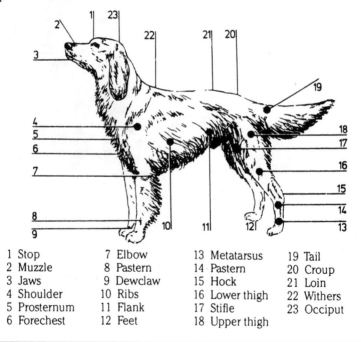

1 Stop	7 Elbow	13 Metatarsus	19 Tail
2 Muzzle	8 Pastern	14 Pastern	20 Croup
3 Jaws	9 Dewclaw	15 Hock	21 Loin
4 Shoulder	10 Ribs	16 Lower thigh	22 Withers
5 Prosternum	11 Flank	17 Stifle	23 Occiput
6 Forechest	12 Feet	18 Upper thigh	

How to Spot African and Asian Elephants

You may think that an elephant is an elephant is an elephant. But if you observe the specimens at the zoo carefully, you will be able to see many differences. If the elephant has a slightly hollowed back, two knobs at the tip of its trunk, large tusks and ears, and is dark gray in color, it is African. If it's smaller, lighter, with a slightly arched back, and one knob at the tip of its trunk, it is Asian.

How to Teach a Bear to Dance

First, make sure it's not a grizzly bear or some other variety that might have a great propensity to turn mean!

North American bears are not usually amenable to training. Your average European bear is a good choice, such as the ones found in Russia. Get your bear young. If you bring the bear up from a cub, it will fixate on you (if you are lucky). Indeed, if you can get a cub at birth and feed it from a bottle, you will form a much stronger bond with it and it will be more obedient and eager to please.

Once the bear is old enough to stand on its own and cavort a little, you simply play music for it and dance with it. Do this in very short spells and always reward the bear with something that it loves to eat, plus lots of praise and affection. Later on, play music and see if the bear will dance. Demonstrate, if necessary, but don't support the bear. If it stares at you in astonishment, put the music on again, and repeat the process. Sooner or later, the bear will get up on its hind legs to the sound of the music. Praise it right away and give it a reward. It will get the idea that the music means it is going to get fed, but ONLY if it gets up on its hind legs and "dances" first.

The method is the one used for training any animal, human or otherwise. It is a form of positive conditioning, as defined by B.F. Skinner, the American behavioral psychologist. Eventually, you can stop giving the bear its food reward every time; give it in an irregular pattern. Because it always hopes to be rewarded, it will respond when it hears the sound of music in the hopes that this will be a time when dancing earns a goodie. From time to time, it will probably also get up and do a little dance just for the hell of it, music or not, in the hope that it will get a little reward. Don't respond, for that could lead to persistent pestering.

How to Ride an Elephant

Ask (politely) the elephant to kneel down on its forelegs. Step up onto its left knee, hold the top of its ear, and climb aboard after gaining a foothold on one of the numerous lumps and bumps along its neck. Straddle the elephant just behind its neck. Grip tightly with your knees, and instead of letting your legs dangle, bend them slightly backwards so that each leg grips the elephant's body along the inside of the calf all the way to the ankle. As the elephant walks, roll your body from side to side with its lumbering motion; this will prevent your backside from getting sore. Do not attempt to ride an elephant in the mating season; at this time, it becomes intractable. Treat the elephant firmly, but with kindness. Elephants do have long memories, and if you abuse one it will remember you and get its own back.

How to Keep a Hedgehog Happy

If you see a hedgehog near your house and want to give it a treat, put out a shallow saucer of bread and milk at night. Hedgehogs also like meat scraps, but these may attract more undesirable animal visitors.

How to Make Friends with a Ferret

Ferrets, the domesticated form of the polecat, are bred for their aggressive hunting instincts. The problem is to handle them safely. A ferret should be handled when it is a four-or-five-week-old kitten and still too small to sink its teeth in. Given a lot of attention and affection at this age, it will be as friendly and as safe to handle as a domestic cat and will only bite in self-defense or because of pain, though it will attack the small furred and feathered creatures which form its natural prey. Young ferrets can be fed on milk and raw meat, but from about three months old should transfer to a meat and water diet. Canned cat and dog food is satisfactory, especially if supplemented with chicken, eggs, mink feed, and extra vitamins.

Ferrets should be inoculated against distemper and, where appropriate, against rabies. Continual handling is necessary to keep them tame.

To test for tameness offer the back of your closed fists for the ferret to sniff: the tight skin will offer no purchase for its teeth (a). If no attempt is made to bite, run your hand gently over the ferrets back (b), grasp the back of its neck (c), and lift it to be carried with both hands (d). Its front feet should protrude between your first and second fingers. Never offer a finger for a ferret to smell, especially a strange one. In parts of the U.S., a permit is needed to keep ferrets because of the damage to poultry if they escape.

How to Milk a Cow

Don't take a bucket out into a field. Bring the cow to where you want to milk her, preferably in a stall eating her food. Speak to her to let her know you're there. Get as close to her back leg as you can when milking, in case you accidently hurt and she kicks. That way she won't hurt you.

Clean her udder with a cloth dipped in water containing a cleansing agent (which you can get from an agricultural specialist).

Then place your hand like a slightly open fist around one of her teats. Squeeze the teat gently with the top fingers, then the lower ones, and repeat in a series of smooth, rippling movements. The milk will spurt out of the teat. Do it slowly until you get used to the movements of the fingers.

If the milk is not white and has yellow curds in it, the teat can be affected by mastitis, and should not be milked. Test all the teats, letting the milk run away. Mastitis is not serious, and it can easily be cured, but the yellow curd would spoil any milk it was mixed with. Now put a clean bucket under the udder and milk in the way described, one teat at a time until the flow stops.

How to Tell an Ape from a Monkey

Apes have arms that are longer than their legs, have no visible tail, and are longer than monkeys. Apes are not indigenous to the New World, but monkeys are, and are also found in Asia and Africa.

How to Feed a Panda

The menu served twice daily to pandas at the National Zoo, Washington DC, consists of four or five carrots, four or five apples, two sweet potatoes, rice mixed with milk and vitamins, 20 lb of bamboo, and two dog biscuits. As between-meal snacks, they are sometimes given honey sandwiches.

How to Hold a Rabbit

Don't pick the rabbit up by it's ears or you may hurt it. You can lift it by the skin at the back of the neck, but immediately support its weight from beneath with your other hand. You can rest its body on your hand and your forearm.

How to Handle a Hamster

An irritable or aggressive hamster can give quite a nip so treat it with respect, and wash the smell of food off your fingers before trying to handle it – or a finger might be confused with dinner! You can lift a hamster by the loose skin of the scruff of the neck, but when it's tame it is better to grasp it firmly around the body and support it on the hand. Avoid sudden movements and noise and always handle the animal gently. There should be no need to wear gloves.

How to Tell a Bactrian Camel from a Dromedary

The two best known members of the camel family are easily distinguished — one has only one hump, the other, two. But which way round is it? Easy, the dromedary is shaped like a letter D on its side, and the bactrian like a letter B.

How to Hunt the Snark

'You may seek it with thimbles – and seek it with care
You may hunt it with forks and hope;
You may threaten its life with a railway share:
You may charm it with smiles and soap. . .

'For the Snark's a peculiar creature, that won't
Be caught in a commonplace way.'

If you want to know what a snark is, read Lewis
Carroll's 'The Hunting of the Snark.'

How to Recognize Mythical Beasts

1 Griffins were huge beasts, with the head and wings of an eagle, the ears of a horse, and the body of a lion. They were often thought to guard a hoard of gold.

2 Unicorns were reputedly a lithe, powerful combination of a horse's body and head with an antelope's legs, a lion's tail, and a fearsome spiral horn on the forehead. Only the virtue of a young maiden could tame a unicorn.

3 Cyclops were man-eating hairy giants with only one eye, set centrally in the forehead. The biggest and most famous cyclops, Polyphemus, lived in a cave and grazed sheep.

4 Satyrs had the torso and head of a man, but the horns and hindquarters of a goat. They were woodland creatures, associated with fertility.

5 Harpies were said to have the head and torso of a woman, pale, thin, with dirty, matted hair, but with the wings and feet of a vulture. They were immortal, although always on the point of starvation.

6 Centaurs had the upper body of a man combined with the body and legs of a horse. They were very civilized, famous for their noble nature and knowledge of medicine.

How to Name an Animal Family

Just as human beings are known as man, woman, or child, according to sex and age, animals have special terms to distinguish them. An adult male swan, for example, is a cob, the female, a pen, and young swans are known as cygnets. Here are some others:

Animal	Male	Female	Juvenile
Kangaroo	buck	doe	joey
Elephant	bull	cow	calf
Lion	lion	lioness	cub
Deer	buck	doe	fawn
Hare	buck	doe	leveret
Tiger	tiger	tiger	cub
Bear	bear	she-bear	cub
Fox	fox	vixen	cub
Pig	boar	sow	piglet
Goat	billy	nanny	kid
Donkey	donkey	jennet	foal

Animal	Male	Female	Juvenile
Dog	dog	bitch	puppy
Sheep	ram	ewe	lamb
Horse	stallion	mare or dam	foal
Cattle	bull	cow	calf
Seal	bull	cow	pup
Whale	bull	cow	calf
Goose	gander	goose	gosling
Duck	drake	duck	duckling
Chicken	cock	hen	chick

How to Keep an Octopus

A small octopus can be kept in a marine aquarium if the conditions are carefully regulated. An octopus prefers slightly alkaline water (pH value 8) kept at a temperature of not more than 71°F (21.6°C). It likes plenty of rocks in which to find hiding places. Its natural food consists of mollusks and crustacea, but it will accept fresh meat.

How to Make Your Candle Fit Your Candlestick

Don't burn it at both ends. If it is a little too large or too loose dip the bottom end about one inch into a bowl of very hot water for a couple of minutes. This will soften the wax and as you press the candle into the holder it will adapt itself to the space available.

How to Measure Humidity

Human hair gets longer in moist air. So one way of measuring humidity is to fasten a long human hair between two points. If the humidity falls, and the air gets drier, the hair will snap. If it becomes loose then the air has become more humid. The greater the humidity of the air the more likely it is to rain.

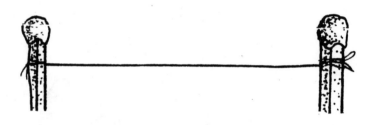

How to Extract a Broken Cork

Use a crochet hook. It's worth keeping one in the house as a tool for getting broken corks out of bottles even though you may never want to crochet!

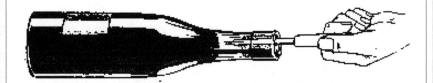

How to Make Candles Last Longer

Coat the outside of the candle with varnish. If you hold them by the wick you can even dip them in a can. The varnish forms a hard coat which will prevent the wax from running down the sides.

How to Stop Rugs from Slipping

One neat, simple, and cheap way is to sew a rubber ring, like the one used on preserve jars, on the underside of the rug at each corner.

How to Sharpen Kitchen Scissors

Cut up sandpaper with them and you will soon put an edge back on the blades.

How to Make Roses Last Longer

Place the stems of the roses up to their necks in hot water for several hours. Before arranging, split or crush the ends of the stems.

How to Tie Packages Tightly

Dip string in warm water before you use it, then tie and knot it in the ordinary way. As the string dries, it will shrink and tighten up.

How to Stop String from Tangling

Put a ball of string into an ordinary plastic funnel, the kind you use for putting liquids into bottles or gasoline into cans. Make sure it is large enough to hold your string. Nail the funnel to the wall or fix it on a bracket at a convenient height. Thread the loose end of the twine through and let the ball rest in the funnel mouth.

How to Heat a Roman Villa

When heating was required in Roman villas, a system known as hypocaust was incorporated. Columns of bricks or tiles separated the floors from the foundations and warm air from central fires circulated through the cavities.

How to Keep Flies Away

Grow basil in pots on your window sill and flies will be discouraged from coming in.

How to Discourage Greenfly

Put garlic among the plants that attract the greenfly.

How to Seat Guests at a Dinner Table

At formal dinner parties in the western world the host and hostess sit at either end of the table, giving it two "heads." The gentleman whom they wish to honor most, or whom they consider most important because of rank, position, or interest, sits on the hostess's right; the lady of greatest honor or importance on the host's right. The places on the side of both host and hostess are assigned to the next most important people and so on to adjoining places down the table. The sexes are placed alternately and men face women across the table if it is an equally mixed guest list, which is what most people aim at. Nowadays, if entertaining privately, formal precedence will give way to the host or hostess's opinion as to who would most interest whom as conversational partners across the table or to the side. At official banquets the rules of rank and diplomatic precedence should be followed. This places the guests of "least importance" in the center of the table, farthest from the host and hostess. In private it is usual for members of the family or close friends of the hosts to be placed among other guests in the center to look after guests who are too far away to be given the host and hostess's attention.

In medieval times, in the household of a king or great lord, the host and his most important guests would be seated at one table, and lesser ranks sat separately. The ceremonial salt, a symbolic rather than a purely functional salt holder which was usually a fine example of the goldsmith or silversmith's art, was placed at the noble man's left. The most important guests sat on his right, although sometimes with quite a wide gap between him and the first guests, especially if there was a big difference in rank. Guests of lesser rank sat on the host's left, below the salt. They were served by a lower grade of servant who did not carry napkins and the gap before their places was greater. Thus "below the salt" came to indicate those not considered important or worthy of a great man's attention.

How to Be a Butler

According to the 19th-century English writer, Mrs Beeton, the duties of the butler in a household were as follows:

1 To supervise all other male servants, to pay the bills, and to run the wine cellar.

2 To serve breakfast, assisted by the footman.

3 To arrange and serve luncheon.

4 At dinner: set out the silverware, announce that the meal is ready, bring in the first dish, carve the meat, and serve the wines. During dessert, he should stand behind the master's chair.

5 At bedtime: bring candles for the household, lock the windows and doors, and see that the fires are in a safe state.

How to Be a Lady's Maid

A lady's maid served the mistress of the household in much the same way that a valet served the master. Mrs. Beeton, the authority on household subjects in 19th-century England, listed these duties for a lady's maid:

1 In the morning, to bring the mistress a cup of tea, and prepare her bath.

2 To check and put away the clothes worn the day before, cleaning them as necessary.

3 To help the mistress dress.

4 To air the bedroom, clean it, and make the bed.

5 To prepare and lay out all changes of clothes required later that day.

In general, the lady's maid should be a capable dressmaker, hairdresser, and adviser on fashions. She would pack for the mistress, accompanying her and performing her usual duties on trips away from home.

How to Be a Valet

Mrs. Beeton, the 19th-century English authority on domestic subjects, lists the following duties of the gentleman's valet:

1 To supervise the master's wardrobe and dressing room, look after all the clothes, seeing to cleaning and repairs, and even select what he will wear.

2 To air and heat the dressing-room, and lay out the clothes in the morning. To sharpen the razor, and prepare hot water and soap for shaving.

3 To cut the master's hair and trim his beard and mustache as necessary.

4 To hand the master his hat, gloves, and cane and open the door when he goes out.

5 To pack the suitcases, and make all the minor arrangements for a journey.

6 Perhaps act as a loader and carry the second gun when the master goes shooting.

How to Protect Your Cutlery

The combination of salt, very hot water, and certain detergents can cause corrosion and pitting even to stainless steel. Don't take the risk: carefully scrape salt from dirty plates before immersing them in dishwater – or better still, wash cutlery separately. Cutlery that is not often used will stay fresh and shiny if, before you store it, you rub it with a cloth soaked with a little olive oil.

How to Remove a Tight Ring

Wet your finger in cold water, rub it with soap, working it under the ring, and then push the ring over the joint, twisting it at the same time.

How to Keep a Silver Teapot Fresh

If you have a silver pot which you use only on special occasions, it may become musty while tucked away in a cupboard. Try grandma's method of leaving a couple of cubes of sugar in the pot to keep it fresh.

How to Clean Stone

Porous stone such as limestone develops a protective crust and if this is removed the stone may crumble. It is best cleaned with a strong jet of water and a stiff brush. Stains are removed by soaking blotting paper in denatured alcohol or turpentine and applying it to the stain until the stain is absorbed by the blotting paper. Mildew is removed by soaking blotting paper in hot distilled water and applying. Non-porous stone such as granite is more robust and can be cleaned with a wire brush and detergent. Denatured alcohol removes oil stains. Clean marble with a solution of soap and water and add half a cup of ammonia per bucket.

How to Polish Stone

Slate and marble can both be polished with an abrasive disk. Pour water onto the stone to act as a lubricant (**1**) and apply the disk in small circular movements (**2**). A suspension will form which should be washed off when the stone is polished sufficiently (**3**). Wax polish is then applied (**4**). Seal slate with a polyurethane varnish. Rinse marble occasionally with a mixture of shellac and denatured alcohol. An abrasive powder should be used for polishing granite. Alabaster should be polished with furniture polish.

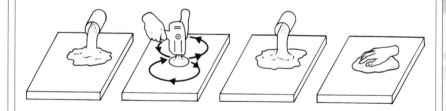

How to Polish Acrylic

Remove the tiny scratches that dull the surface by rubbing with a soft rag that has a little metal polish on it. Finish polishing with a clean rag.

How to Clean a Burned Saucepan

Fill the pan with cold water into which you have put a tablespoonful of vinegar, and boil for 5 minutes. This should deal with minor burning.

How to Clean Patent Leather

Rub gently with a cloth dipped in almond oil. Polish with a soft, dry cloth.

How to Remove Cigarette Stains

If nicotine-stained fingers reveal that you've not kicked the habit, rub them with a piece of lemon or with cotton dipped in hydrogen peroxide. Rinse in water immediately afterward.

How to Handle a Ladder

The basic principle when using ladders is never to take risks: no old ladders, damaged rungs, or improvised supports should be used. Place the base of the ladder against the wall (**1**) and walk forward from the other end underneath the ladder raising it to a vertical position (**2**). Pull out the base until the distance is one fourth of the height (**3**). Use both hands when climbing (**4**). If the ladder wobbles, check the base and rest. On soft ground secure the base on a board (**5**) and on hard ground block with a heavy sack (**6**). Do not lean the ladder against glass or fragile materials. Window cleaners' ladders have a padded cross piece to spread the weight if they have to be leaned against plate glass (**7**). Try not to lean out beyond the ladder. The general rule is to keep your hips between the rails (**8**). Never stand on the top four rungs (**9**). If you cannot reach, then use an extension ladder.

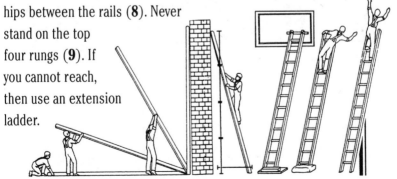

How to Hit a Nail on the Head

Hold the hammer at the end, rather than in the middle, and keep your eye on the nail. Tap the nail gently at first so it stands on its own; then, from the elbow, deliver firm strokes, keeping the wrist straight.

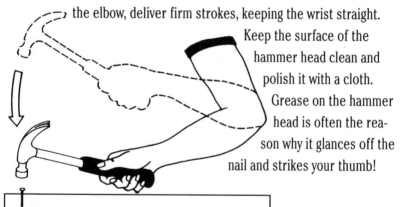

Keep the surface of the hammer head clean and polish it with a cloth. Grease on the hammer head is often the reason why it glances off the nail and strikes your thumb!

How to Keep a Nail from Splitting Wood

If you wipe the nail on a piece of soap, or draw it through your hair just before using it, it is less likely to split the wood into which you hammer it.

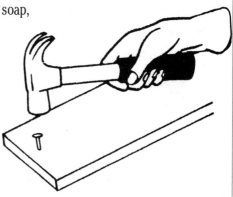

How to Tighten a Loose Screw

Wrap some wire wool around the thread. Then tighten the screw. It should hold tight.

How to Mend Stone

Stone can be joined with an epoxy resin. The edges should be rubbed down with coarse glass-paper and cleaned with a detergent and water. Dry them, and then apply the adhesive. Chips in marble can be masked by building up with a mixture of epoxy resin and whiting, colored appropriately.

How to Glaze a Window

Remove every scrap of broken glass, putty, and sprigs (the small nails that hold the glass in place) using a hammer, chisel, and pliers as necessary. Brush the woodwork to remove any tiny leftover fragments. Make a bed for the new glass with fresh putty, squeeze it around the frame with your thumb and forefinger, and press firmly in all around, pressing on the edges not the center. Push the glass into place. Tap in sprigs 9 in (23 cm) apart to hold the glass in position and then press more putty firmly around the edges of the pane. Using a putty knife (or you could make do with a penknife), produce a neat bevel corresponding to that of neighboring panes. Trim off any excess on the glass and neatly miter the corners. Allow the putty to dry for a week or so and then paint over it. Metal-frame windows are glazed in the same way but special clips are used instead of sprigs and a special putty must be used. It is also wise to take the opportunity to treat the metal with an anti-rust preparation before putting in the bedding putty.

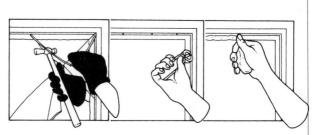

How to Coat a Paintbrush

Too much paint on your brush will lead to uneven application, run back into the roots of the bristles, and even spread onto the handle. Make sure that you fill your brush evenly and well. Stretch a thin wire across the top of the open paint can. If the can has a handle you can attach it to its ends, or to a circle of wire below the edge, or tape it on. Every time you load your brush with paint wipe it against this wire and excess paint will drip back into the can. That saves paint, mess, and trouble.

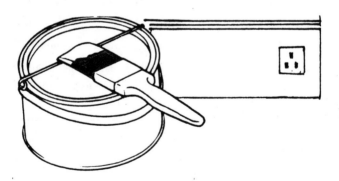

How to Check the Engine of a Used Car

Remove the cap from where you add oil to the engine and place your palm over the opening. Rev the engine. If the seals and gaskets are in good condition you will feel suction on your palm. Then scoop out some oil from just inside the rim and rub it between your fingers. If the oil feels gritty, the engine, sooner or later, is going to give you trouble. Take great care not to put your hands near any moving parts.

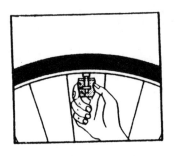

How to Repair a Flat Bicycle Tire

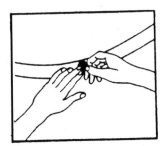

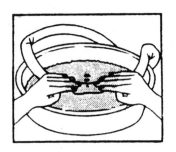

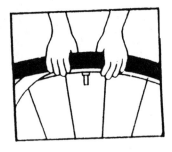

First check the outside of the tire for any sharp objects stuck in it that may have caused the puncture, or any gashes in the tire. Note or mark any such position. If no indication of a puncture is apparent, reinflate the tire and check the valve. You may be able to feel air escaping, but if not, place the valve at the top of the wheel, and immerse it in water (**1**). If it is leaking, renew the rubber or replace. If the valve is satisfactory, remove the wheel and unscrew the valve. Starting opposite the valve, insert tire levers between the tire and the rim and lever one side of the tire off (**2**). Then pull the inner tube out. Replace the valve and inflate the tube, and check for leaks by squeezing the tube and passing it slowly through a bowl of water (**3**) and watch for air escaping. Check the whole tube for punctures – there may be more than one – and mark them; a wax crayon is best for this. Deflate the tube and clean up the puncture area with glass paper. Spread adhesive over the area, and when tacky apply the patch (**4**). Dust with chalk. Replace the tube and insert the valve. Slightly inflate the tube and tuck it into the tire. Press the tire over the rim (**5**), starting opposite the valve, making sure that the tube is not pinched. Then inflate the tire fully.

How to Stop a Creaking Stair

The ghostly creaks and squeaks are probably caused by the top surface of the tread rubbing against the bottom of the riser. A nail or two driven at an angle down through the tread and into the bottom of the riser should stop the movement and silence the creak.

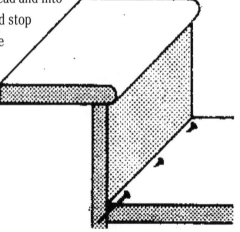

How to Make a Wrench Smaller

If a wrench cannot be adjusted any tighter and is still too big, make it fit by inserting a coin between one jaw of the wrench and the nut you are trying to turn.

How to Make Buttons Stay on Longer

Paint nail polish over the crossed threads of the buttons, both front and back.

How to Tie a Bow Tie

The tie may have shaped (A) or straight ends, but the method is the same for both. Left and right refer to your own left and right if you are tying a tie on yourself.

Put the tie around your neck and cross the right end over and under the left end (B) leaving a full bow width on the left end facing front, double a length behind it to halfway along the bow (D). Double back the end as you did in (B) and tuck the doubled part into the space between the folded left end and the fabric around your neck, pushing from left to right and leaving the actual end to the right (E).

This forms the basic bow which you can now adjust until it is smooth and neat (F). At first you may find that the lengths at the sides of the bow are disproportionate or that the whole tie is too loose. With practice, you will get the balance of the bow just right. If the overall tie is too loose, you should shorten the tie. Obviously, this must be done in the center to avoid having to reshape the ends; many ties have an adjustable center to facilitate this.

How to Fold a Suit for Packing

Jacket Lay it flat on its back, bring the two fronts together, and fasten one button. Lay the upper part of the sleeves parallel with the sides of the jacket, then fold over at the elbows so that the sleeves cross on the "chest." Fold the bottom of the jacket upward from the waist to lie flat over the sleeves and the upper part.

Pants Lay flat, with one leg on top of the other so that the front and back creases align. There's no need to do up the fly, but make sure all pockets are flat. Then fold the legs over from the cuffs upward, either in half or in three depending on the size of your suitcase, and lay them on top of the jacket.

How to Bull Your Boots

You need a cloth, boot polish, spit, and plenty of energy. With the cloth apply a generous layer of polish to the boots, spit on them, and rub the spit and polish well into the leather – hence the expression "spit and polish." Some people spit into the polish can instead, and others cheat and melt polish over their boots and burnish it with a smooth bone, the handle of a toothbrush, or a spoon. "Bull" is British army slang for polishing, cleaning, and ceremonial drill. Bulling your boots to put a shine on the toecaps you can see to shave in looms large in the life of a new recruit, but by burnishing away the natural grain of the leather it can damage the leather and shorten the life of the boots so it is actually discouraged in wartime.

How to Wear a Kilt

First, are you entitled to wear a particular tartan – the woven, check-like pattern of the fabric? Each highland clan has its own design and colors, though they are not necessarily of great antiquity. If you are not a Scot or of Scottish ancestry there are many to choose from, although you will run the risk of offending purists who consider you should not wear a tartan but some other plaid, and that you probably ought not to wear a kilt at all. The original highland "belted plaid" was a mantle 6 feet wide by 12-18 feet long (1.8 x 4-5 m) which was laid on the ground and folded into pleats until its length was reduced to about 5 feet (1.5 m) with one end unpleated to cover the front of the body. The wearer lay upon it, the lower edge level with his knees, folded it around him, fastened it around the waist with a leather belt, and threw the remaining plaid over his shoulder. The modern kilt is just the lower part of the "belted plaid," with two sets of buckles sewn at either end of a length of fabric that wraps around the waist. This must be long enough to cover the bottom of the knees. Place one end of the fabric on the hip, buckles uppermost, and wind it across in front and then behind you. Push the buckle straps through the slots in the fabric that should now cover them, and do them up. The remaining fabric goes across your front and buckles on the other hip. Over the kilt you should wear a sporran, a sort of purse threaded to a belt that is slung on the hips, purse to the front protecting the crotch, as it were. It can be either of plain leather with plain tassels, or it can be much more decorative, trimmed with fur and silver. Either way, it is an extremely convenient place to keep your credit cards and whiskey miniatures. Now for your vest and jacket. These are specially designed for wear with the kilt and can be either informal and tweedy-looking or more formal and black. Any old jacket will not do. Shirts should be plain-colored, preferably white. Ties should also be plain or tartan. For formal occasions, try a lace bib. To finish off: socks must be calf-length and be of plain, heavy wool. An optional extra is the dirk, a small dagger. This is worn inside one of the socks, handle protruding at the top of the calf. Shoes? That is up to you. You can buy the special shoes that are suited to formal occasions. Otherwise, plain shoes or brogues, rather than high-fashion shoes, are best. As for what you wear underneath your kilt. Well, that would be telling, wouldn't it?

How to Wear a Toga

The loose toga, worn by the Romans as a symbol of honor, was a large curved piece of fabric worn over closer-fitting undergarments. It was draped over the left shoulder and across the back, then brought under the right arm and flung over the left arm and shoulder.

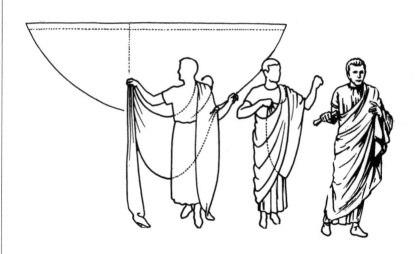

How to Wear a Sari

The traditional Indian sari is made from a rectangle of fabric about 18 ft long, and it is worn over a close fitting short-sleeved bodice. The fabric is wrapped once round the body, then most of the rest of the free end is folded back and forth in pleats (**1**) and tucked into the waist at the front (**2**). The last part of the fabric is wrapped round the body and over the left shoulder (**3**).

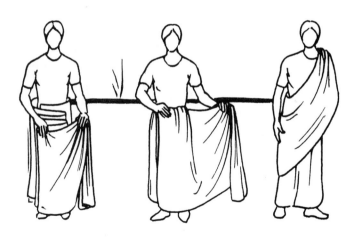

How to Dance the Hora

This popular Israeli dance originated in the Balkans. It is danced in a circle with the dancers holding hands, linked handkerchiefs, or with arms extended on their neighbors' arms. It begins at a reasonably slow tempo and gradually gets faster and faster. Steps are the same for all dancers.

1 Step to the left with the left foot. Cross the right foot behind the left foot and step.

2 Step to the left with the left foot, hop on the same foot at the same time swinging the right foot across in front of it.

3 Step in place with the right foot, hop on the right foot while swinging the left foot in front of it.

The dance may also be done in the opposite direction, or in alternate directions, in which case the following steps are performed at the end of movement in each direction. Jump lightly once, hold. Jump a second time, hold. Then make three jumps in succession, followed by one hold before moving sideways in the opposite direction.

How to Seat an Orchestra

The players in an orchestra are not seated randomly. The conductor needs the instrumentalists of each type grouped together, so that they can all see the signals he or she gives them, and the groups are placed to give the best sound balance for the work or works being played. Individual concert halls and even specific pieces may require variations on the basic plan but the usual arrangement of the players is shown here

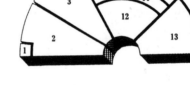

1 Harp

2 1st Violins

3 2nd Violins

4 Side drum
　Bass drum
　Timpani

5 Tam-tam
　Cymbals
　Xylophone
　Glockenspiel
　Tubular bells

6 Horns

7 Trumpets
　Trombones
　Tuba

8 Clarinets
　Bass clarinets

9 Bassoons
　Contra bassoons

10 Piccolo
　Flutes

11 Oboe
　Cor anglais

12 Violas

13 Cellos

14 Double basses

How to Play the Comb and Paper

Take an ordinary pocket comb, and put it in a fold of stiff tissue paper. Then hum through it, holding it against your slightly parted lips.

How to Play the Castanets

A pair of castanets consists of two pieces of hollowed hardwood, linked by a cord threaded through two holes in each piece. You wind the cord around the thumb and click the two plates together with your fingers. Place a pair of castanets in each hand. The left hand pair plays a simple rhythm, while with the right hand you perform the full complicated rhythm of the dance. Don't be too dismayed if you aren't as good as a Spanish dancer; the great percussionist James Blades said, "The superb artistry of the Spanish player defies imitation."

How to Blow a Hunting Horn

You blow a hunting horn through a cup-shaped mouthpiece like an alp horn, but you have to keep your lips tighter and blow harder. You can't really pitch a note on a hunting horn, so you get a series of upward swoops. Each huntsman has his own calls to signal to hounds. A series of repeated "whoop-whoop-whoops" generally indicates that the pack has "gone away" in pursuit of the fox.

How to Play an Alp Horn

An alp horn is a wind instrument up to 13 feet (4 meters) long, with a wooden cup-shaped mouthpiece. It produces a series of harmonic sounds (not a true musical scale) and only a limited range of tunes can be played. To blow it you need to press your lips against the mouthpiece and, keeping the lips slightly tensed, blow gently into it. The varying tension of the lips and the amount you blow produce different notes. You probably won't be able to do it easily if you have dentures.

How to Play the Bagpipes

This is a very ancient type of instrument and is known in many different forms around the world, but they all use the same principle. It consists of an inflatable bag, originally an animal's skin, into which air can be blown through a mouth pipe. From it also protrude a number of drone pipes which produce sound of a continuous pitch, and one or more pipes with finger stops on which the melody can be played. Squeezing the bag drives air through the pipes to produce the sound, which is not interrupted by the player having to breathe.

How to Play the Teacups

Take a number of teacups of different sizes and thicknesses, and tie each individually to a line stretched between two uprights. Strike them with a spoon or stick. Keep any cups which produce a good note and replace the others with new cups until you have the scale or range of notes that you require. The British composer Benjamin Britten, when visiting schools in East Anglia to choose singers and instrumentalists to appear in his *Noyes Fludde*, was so impressed with a schoolboy who had made himself such an instrument, that he wrote a special part for it and the young musician in his lively setting of this medieval version of the Old Testament story. It perfectly matches the raindrops falling at the beginning of the storm and the heavy rain in the storm.

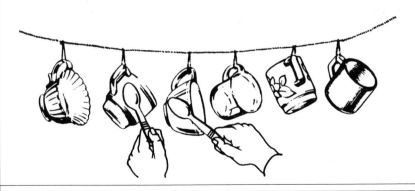

How to Play the Spoons

Choose a pair of heavy spoons, and hold them, bowl to back, between the middle finger and the thumb with the forefinger between them, so that they can pivot and the bowl of one can clap into the bowl of the other. You can use them as a pair of clappers by bouncing them off your knee, or rub them up and down the folds in your coat sleeve to get a trilling effect.

How to Confuse Your English

Though it's the same basic language, American (and much of Canadian) English can be quite different from English as it is spoken in England. For instance, if you go into Woolworth's in London, England, and ask for thumb tacks they won't know what to give you; anymore than if you go into Woolworth's in London, Ontario, or Oxford, Mississippi, and ask for drawing pins. They are, of course, the same thing. An American hangs his clothes up in the closet, but an English person uses a wardrobe or cupboard. In America, the law enjoins you (i.e. forbids you) from spitting on the sidewalk; while in England, the law enjoins you to drive on the left hand side of the road (i.e. compels or requires you to do so). You can get into a lot of trouble if you don't know some of the different usages. For instance, if your friend lives on the first floor in New York, he or she lives on the ground floor, or the floor that is the same as the one with the entrance. In England, someone living on the first floor lives on what Americans would consider to be the second floor. English people, in common with other Europeans, begin with the ground floor and call the next floor up the first floor and so on. Here are some more examples of words that could lead to embarrassment or misunderstanding:

American English	British English
Purse	Handbag
Coin purse	Purse
Pants	Trousers
Underpants	Pants
Vest	Waistcoat
Undershirt	Vest
Rummage sale	Jumble sale
Zee (Z)	Zed
Monkey wrench	Spanner
Zip code	Post code
Truck	Lorry
Checkers	Draughts
Diapers	Nappies
Elevator	Lift
Kerosene	Paraffin
Gas	Petrol
Drugstore	Chemist (and they don't serve refreshment)

And for some more that mean something different:

Mad American: angry; British: crazy, insane.

Mason American: worker in brick or stone; British: only in stone.

Char American: to burn; British: to burn, but also to clean for someone else, and as a noun, a house cleaner. **Sack** American: bed, as in "hit the sack"; British: to fire from a job (and a coarse cloth bag in both)

Nosh American: a snack between meals; British: a big, slap-up meal as in "nosh-up."

Measures differ too:

	American
Gallon	231 cubic inches
Pint	28.87 cubic inches liquid measure (16oz)
	33.6 cubic inches dry measure
Quart	57.8 cubic inches liquid measure (32oz)
	67.2 cubic inches dry measure
Ton	2000 pounds = a short ton in Britain
Billion	1 thousand million (1,000,000,000)
Trillion	1 million million (1,000,000,000,000)
Quadrillion	1 million billion (1,000,000,000,000,000)

How to Tell Linear A from Linear B

Linear A and Linear B are two very similar scripts found on clay tablets in the ruins of the ancient Cretan civilization at Knossos. Scholars found that Linear B inscriptions are in an early form of Greek. Linear A, the older script, is in a different language which hasn't yet been identified. To the casual eye the two scripts look alike, but the lines of writing on Linear B tablets are separated by rules or guidelines, while there are no such rules on Linear A tablets. Nearly two-thirds of the Linear B symbols are almost identical to those of Linear A, while the rest have no equivalent. Note: The scripts are called linear because they're written in lines.

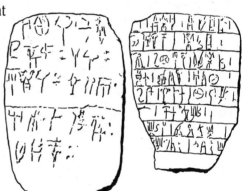

How to Read an Alchemist's Formula

The alchemists of the Middle Ages tried for centuries to make gold from less valuable minerals. If you ever find one of their recipes, you will need to understand the symbols used. But don't get excited – none of the concoctions worked.

How to Read the Secrets of Leonardo da Vinci

The artist and scientist Leonardo da Vinci made thousands of drawings and observations in his notebooks, recording details of shape and form and his ideas for inventions, but his notes appear to be made in a secret code. Leonardo was left handed and his writing goes from right to left. Hold it up in front of a mirror and you will be able to read it in the reflection – if your Italian is good enough!

How to Recognize Classical Columns

The Ancient Greeks devised three main styles of architecture, most easily recognized by the different capitals on their columns, although the fluting of the columns, the arrangement of the base, and the entablature (the bands of moldings above the columns) all differ in their pure form. These three styles are the Doric, the Ionic, and the Corinthian. The Romans adopted the Greek forms but also devised another version of the Doric, often known as the Tuscan order, and an elaborate combination of the Ionic and Corinthian shapes in the Composite order. Classical architects and builders also noticed that if a column is built of exactly the same diameter through all its length it does not look right. An optical illusion of an inward curve appears. To correct this appearance they gave a convex curve to columns, whether cylindrical or tapering, a technique known as entasis.

How to Recognize a Greek Vase

Greek vases were made in a number of basic shapes, each matched to its purpose so well that they were seldom varied.

1 The krater: a wide-mouthed container for mixing wine and water.

(A) Column krater (B) Volute krater (C) Calyx krater

2 The amphora: a large urn used for storing supplies. This might also have a pointed base for sticking in sand or soft earth.

3 The hydria: for carrying water, with two handles placed for easy lifting and with a third handle for pouring.

4 The oenochoe: a pitcher, the standard vessel for serving wine.

5 The kylix: a two-handed drinking cup.

6 The lekythos: an oil jar.

How to Classify Boxers

There are eight classes for professional and Olympic boxers, ten for amateurs outside the Olympics. All are based solely on weight – height, reach, and other statistics are not taken into account. The weights given are the heaviest for each class.

Boxing class weight limits:

CLASS	AIBA
Light flyweight	105.8 lb
Flyweight	112.4 lb
Bantamweight	119.0 lb
Super bantamweight	
Featherweight	125.7 lb
Junior lightweight	
Lightweight	132.3 lb
Light welterweight	140.0 lb
Welterweight	147.7 lb
Light middleweight	156.5 lb
Middleweight	165.3 lb
Light heavyweight	178.6 lb
Heavyweight	greater than 178.6 lb

How to Swim the Butterfly

The butterfly stroke was first developed in the 1930s but not recognized for competitive swimming until 1953, when it was known as the butterfly breast stroke. It was a development of the breast stroke with bent elbows flapping out of the water like fluttering wings. It is a difficult and exhausting stroke to execute but is second only to the crawl in speed. For the leg kick, both legs move together to give an up and down motion like a dolphin's tail. There are two leg beats to one arm stroke. Breathing, which can be either with the head turned to one side as in the crawl or with the head kept forward and lifted out of the water, always takes place at the end of the arm pull and the second kick of the legs.

1 arms enter water in line with shoulder; legs kick downward
2 feet should be straight and level with body; hips rise to surface
3 hands press out and down, elbows bend and keep high
4 hands nearly meet under chest
5 legs complete down beat movement
6 arms leave water, legs move upward without bending

7 arms meet above the water, head is lowered, feet almost break surface at the start of second kick

8 swimmer exhales as arms pull

9 arms finish their pull, second kick is made, breath is taken

10 arms meet above water, head is lowered face down

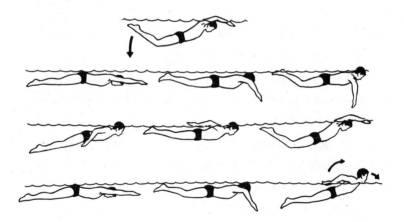

How to Get Up on Water Skis

Make sure the skis are properly fitted. Grasp the tow rope and lean slightly backward, but with the head foreward and the knees bent under your body. The tips of the skis should be protruding above the surface of the water.

As the boat moves away, and the slack of the rope is taken up, move from crouching to an upright position. Keep your arms straight and do not let the boat pull you foward; resist its pull with the muscles in your back and legs. Don't worry if you do not succeed the first time. Getting started is probably the hardest part of water skiing.

If you fall – and everyone does at sometime or other – let go of the tow rope immediately, tuck your head in and bring your knees up to your chest so that you roll into a ball and fall backward if you can. When you've recovered, you can release the skis if it is difficult maneuvering with them in the water.

How to Throw a Discus

Competitive discus throwing is done in a circular motion, like that used for hammer throwing. The discus is made of wood or similar material with a metal rim. For men, the discus must weigh at least 4 lb 6.5 oz and for women 2 lb 3.2 oz. Discus throwing was popular in classical times both for exercise and in competition, as Greek and Roman statues indicate. The ancient discus was usually made of stone. Today the thrower may hold and throw the discus in any way he or she likes, but the usual method is to rest the index finger on the rim and to curl the other fingers around the edge with the thumb and palm supporting the discus against the pull of centrifugal force as it is swung by the thrower. To gain momentum the thrower will raise the discus from a low to a high position, twisting the body or even running in a circle, releasing it at the top of its curve and making it spin forward as it leaves the hand.

How to Throw a Hammer

If you want to throw a hammer in competitive athletics don't go to your tool box – for the modern Olympic hammer is nothing like the tool. It is a spherical head of hard metal, or a shell of such metal filled with lead or other material attached to a length of steel wire at the end of which is either a single or a double grip. The minimum total weight is 16 lb. Competitors usually wear a glove on the hand which comes in contact with the wire grip. Keeping within a 7-foot circle, you begin with the sphere on the ground and turn to swing it up into the air, releasing your grip when the momentum developed will carry it farthest. Its release must be within a 40° arc and it must land within that arc. The distance is measured from the nearest mark made by the sphere when it lands to the inner edge of the ring bounding the throwing circle. In competition the winner is the best after six trials.

How to Tie a Karate Belt

1 Wrap the belt around the body from the front.

2 Loop end (a) over and under end (b) as shown.

3 Loop end (b) back and thread end (a) up through it as shown.

4 Pull ends (a) and (b) tight to complete the knot.

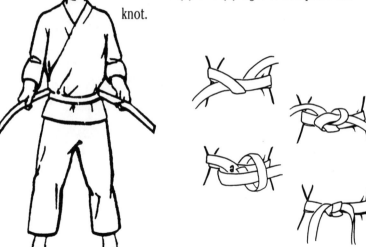

How to Throw a Boomerang

A boomerang is a form of throwing stick, used as a hunting weapon. Its airfoil shape carries it much further than a plain throwing stick of the same size and weight because its contour gives it lift. The wings rotate, giving the boomerang stability, and they present only a small angle to the airflow, thus reducing air resistance. Throw an ordinary boomerang in the plane of rotation, almost horizontally, so that it spins through the air. The lifting force then acts in a direction opposite to that of gravity. You'll need a lot of practice before you can hit what you are aiming at. A return boomerang is used much less often, although that is the kind that comes to mind when most people

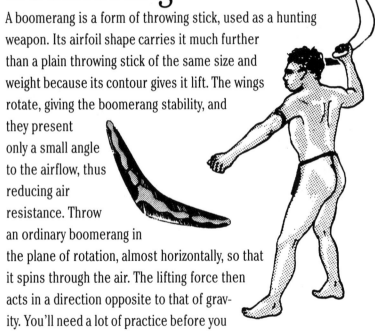

hear the word. They are sometimes used for hunting but are more frequently used for frightening birds so that they will fly into the hunters'
nets. A return boomerang is thrown vertically and its trajectory turns to
the left. Boomerangs are not restricted to the Australian aborigines. They
were used for hunting in southern and north western India, and among
the Hopi people of North America, and were used by the ancient
Egyptians, and in prehistoric Europe.

How to Remove a Dent from a Ping-Pong Ball

Put it in hot water – you'll have to hold it down. The expansion of the air inside will gradually push the skin back into shape, provided it is not actually cracked.

How to Find a Perfect Number

To see whether a number is perfect, find all the numbers that can be exactly divided into it. Add them together; if the total is the original number, that number is perfect. There are only three perfect numbers under 500; they are 6, 28, and 496.

How to Make an Icosahedron

Copy the shape drawn here; it is made up from 20 equilateral triangles. Score along the straight lines with a compass point, fold into shape, and glue the edges into place to form a perfect regular icosahedron.

How to Measure a Mile

We get our word from the Latin *mille* (one thousand) and it had its origin in the Roman army. The standard pace of the Roman legionnaire was two strides, making a measure of about five feet. When he had taken 1000 paces he had marched about 5000 ft, not far off the 5280 ft of a modern mile. The pace was not the only measure based on the human body to provide a rough and ready measure available to everyone. The cubit was the length of a man's forearm from the elbow to the tip of the middle finger, and was divided into palms and digits, and we all know about feet. Gradually these measurements became standardized. The Romans fixed the cubit at the equivalent of 26.6 inches, and that was divided into two feet, each 12 inches long.

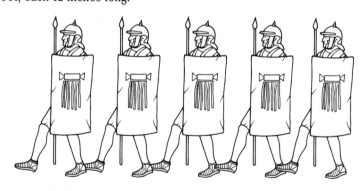

How to Count in Roman Numerals

The Roman numeral system consists of seven numbers represented by seven capital letters: I = 1, V = 5, X = 10, L = 50, C = 100, D = 500, M = 1000. Most numbers use the principle of addition, for instance XI = 10 + 1 = 11, but 4s and 9s use subtraction, so IV = 5 − 1 = 4, IX = 10 − 1 = 9. So the numbers from 1 to 20 are I, II, III, IV, V, VI, VII, VIII, IX, X, XI, XII, XIII, XIV, XV, XVI, XVII, XVIII, XIX, XX. Working in the same way with the higher numbers, 40 = XL (50 − 10), 60 = LX (50 + 10), 90 = XC (100 − 10), 110 = CX (100 + 10). To write a more complex number, for example 3625, start with MMM (3 x 1000), add DC (500 + 100) and XXV (10 + 10 + 5) and the result is MMMDCXXV. To avoid very large numerals, a bar, or vinculum, drawn over the figure indicates that it is multiplied by 1000, so $\overline{\text{MMMMM}}$ = 5000 x 1000 = 5,000,000.

How to Build a Sandcastle

The design is up to you but there are three basic ways of handling the sand.

Simple method Build a form with handfuls of sand, patting it into shape. Fill a bucket with sand, tamp it down with a shovel and turn out to make towers.

Wet method Fill your bucket with sopping wet sand. Scoop it out in your hands and let it drip through your fingers to form fantastic towers, spires, and surreal mounds. Not much use for making solid, architectural forms, which require compacted sand to stay firm.

Sand sculpture Makes mound of compacted sand—you can create basic forms to work with by filling a large four-sided wooden box with wet sand pressing on it with shovel and feet until it is compacted and firm enough to turn out as a solid block. Now carve it into shape. Start off with shovels and trowels and then work on with smaller instruments, pen knives, and nail files!

How to Draw a Triangle with Three Right Angles

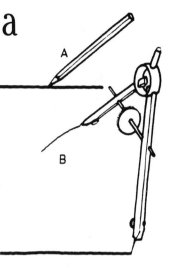

Everyone is taught in school that a triangle can have only one right angle. However, if you take a sphere you can draw a triangle on it with three perfect right angles, as shown.

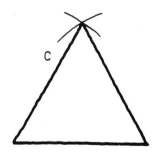

How to Read Chinese Numerals

The following symbols are the chinese characters used for numbers 1 to 10.

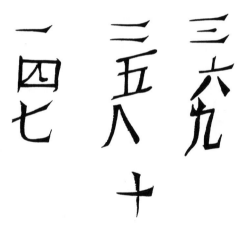

How to Draw a Hexagon

Use a pair of compasses to draw a circle (A). Keeping the compasses at the same radius, place the point anywhere on the circle and mark a point where the pencil touches the circumference (B). Place the point on that mark, and do the same all the way around the circle (C). You will be able to do this exactly six times. Join up the six marks on the circumference and you will have formed a hexagon (D).

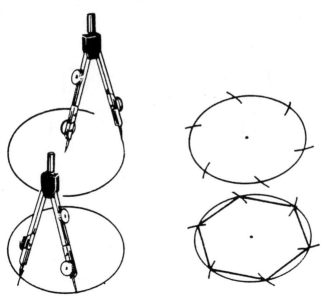

How to Convert Inches to Centimeters

Multiply the inches by 2.54 to find the equivalent number of centimeters.
Multiply centimeters by 0.3937 to find the equivalent in inches.

$$in \times 2.54 = cm$$
$$cm \times 0.3937 = in$$

How to Calculate Compound Interest

In compound interest, the principal (the amount of original money invested) is increased by the amount of interest earned, as happens in a bank savings account. There is a formula for calculating this. You need to know:

P the principal

T the time invested

R the amount for one unit invested plus the interest earned over one unit of time: ($1 at 5% per annum = 1.05)

The amount accruing over a period will then be P x R^T

For example: to find the compound interest on $460 invested over 4 years at 9% per annum (R = 1.09)

P x R^T = $460 (1.09 x 1.09 x 1.09 x 1.09) = 460 x 1.4115816 = $649.32753

Take away the original sum ($460) and the total interest earned = $189.32753.

How to Convert Centigrade to Fahrenheit

(and back again)

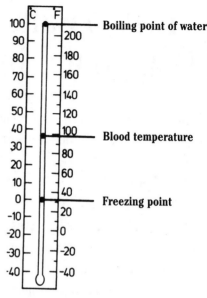

Gabriel Daniel Fahrenheit, born in Danzig (now Gdansk), developed his thermometer scale in 1714. Centigrade was devised in 1742 by Anders Celsius, a Swede. Although Centigrade remains a popularly accepted name for the 100-based scale, it was officially renamed Celsius, in honor of its originator, by an international conference in 1948. There are exactly 100 (0°-100°) degrees on a Celsius thermometer between the temperature points at which water will freeze and boil, and 180 degrees (32°-212°) on the Fahrenheit scale. To convert one to the other apply the following formula:

Centigrade to Fahrenheit: $(F = \frac{9C}{5} + 32)$.

Multiply the Centigrade temperature by 9 then divide by 5 and add 32. Thus boiling point of 100°C becomes 9 x 100 = 900 divided by 5 = 180 plus 32 = 212°F.

Fahrenheit to Centigrade: $(C = \frac{F-32}{9} \times 5)$.

Deduct 32 from the Fahrenheit temperature, divide by 9, and multiply the result by 5. Thus boiling point 212° − 32 = 180 which divided by 9 is 20 which multiplied by 5 equals 100°C. Normal blood heat (for humans) is 98.6°F or 37°C.

How to Make Egg Paint

Tempera (or egg paint) was the usual medium before the introduction of oil colors in the fifteenth century and it is still used today. Some painters use only the egg yolks, others only the whites, some a mixture. It dries very quickly, almost immediately after application, and forms a very tough surface. This is a recipe used by Austrian monks:

   4 eggs

   1 teaspoon linseed oil

   1 teaspoon vinegar

Break the eggs into a jar (a). Cap and shake the jar (b) mixing well together. Add oil and vinegar and shake again until thoroughly mixed. Strain through muslin. Mix in pigment as required (c). Use rapidly.

How to Make a Quill Pen

Use one of the largest wing feathers of a bird, such as a goose, turkey, or crow. Heat sand in a pan until very hot. Remove from heat and place the end of the quill in the sand for a few minutes. This will dry the oils and harden the quill. Dissolve a little salt in boiling water. Now, dip the end of the quill in this. With a knife, cut the end of the quill at an oblique angle to form a writing point, making a vertical slit to complete the "nib."

How to Make Invisible Ink

There are several recipes for making invisible inks.

1 Dissolve 1 part of cobalt chloride and 1 part of gum arabic in 8 parts of water. Messages written in this ink show up in blue when the paper is heated.

2 Dissolve 10 grains of nickel chloride and 10 grains of cobalt chloride in 1 oz of water. This ink turns green when heated.

3 Use rice water as ink. The writing will show up when it is brushed over with tincture of iodine.

4 Write in milk. The writing will show up if you rub a dirty finger over it. This method has been used by prisoners to write messages between the lines of otherwise innocuous letters.

How to Keep Ink from Smearing in the Rain

How often have you found the writing on a letter smudged by rain as you've gone out to mail it? Use old candle ends to avoid this annoyance. Rub the wax over the writing and it will provide a waterproof covering. Don't use this just for letters and packages, it's very useful for garden labels too.

How to Make a Brass Rubbing

You will need:

Architect's or draftsman's detail paper (preferably) or decorator's lining paper.

Stick of heelball (originally produced for cobblers, it is a compound of beeswax, tallow, and lampblack).

Weights or masking tape.

First obtain permission from the owner, or the clergyman or caretaker if the brass you wish to make a rubbing of is in a church or public building. Ensure that your paper is wide enough to cover all the brass to be rubbed (you can join the paper but it makes rubbing more difficult). Clean the brass with a cloth and soft brush to remove grit and dust, which may tear the paper, and then carefully position the paper. If the brass is on the

floor, weight the corners to prevent the paper moving. On some surfaces masking tape may be used to stretch and hold the paper in position but beware it may damage soft plaster or stone. If it is not possible to secure the paper, great care must be taken that it does not move during rubbing. An assistant to hold it will help. If the brass is an outline shape remember its position. With a firm and even movement, rub the heelball over the area of the brass and an image will appear. You can either restrict your rubbing to the brass itself or with practice you will be able to follow the edge of the metal quite easily or rub across the whole slab of stone on which it is mounted. The latter method will enable you to record the position of missing pieces of brass as well. Use only a moderate pressure over such areas and a circular motion. Before removing the paper make sure you have not omitted any details.

How to Copy a Picture Carved on Stone

A stone rubbing can be made in a similar way to a brass rubbing (see p.232) but an alternative method is to make a dabbing. Mix powdered graphite with linseed oil into a paste on a board (a). Make a pad from fine cloth wrapped around a ball of cotton (b). Dip the pad in the paste (c), remove surplus and apply it with moderate pressure to the surface of the paper (d). Very little friction is created by this method so much thinner paper, even tissue paper, can be used. This method also works well for very intricate brasses.

How to Make Beads from Paper

Cut strips of paper, glue them on one side, and roll them round a knitting needle. When they are dry, slip them off, paint them, and string them into jewelry.

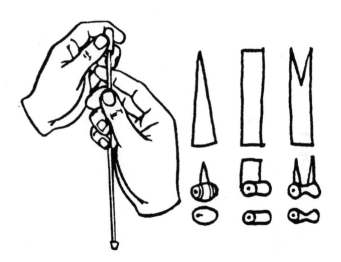

How to Thread Beads Easily

Dip the end of the twine in nail polish or rub it with soap. This will stiffen it. Lay the beads in a row on a piece of corrugated cardboard and you can push the twine through a row at a time – this only works with beads of equal size.

How to Rake Small Leaves

If you use a big wire rake small leaves often seem to slip through the prongs. You can prevent this by threading a strip of cardboard or plastic between the prongs just wide enough to block all except the last ½ inch (13 mm) of their length.

How to Bottle a Whole Pear

As a piece of gamesmanship, produce an after-dinner bottle of pear flavored brandy, with a full-sized pear mysteriously intact inside the small-necked bottle. The secret lies in tying an empty bottle to a branch of a pear tree so that it encloses a blossom; with luck this will set into a fruit that will grow and ripen. When ripe, break the pear off at the stem and fill up the bottle with brandy; leave it for some months to mingle flavors.

How to Take a Cutting

Hardwood cuttings (forsythia, roses, gooseberries, currents, etc.)
Take cuttings in early autumn. Select a mature side shoot, about 12 in long and low on the plant. Pull it from the stem so that the heel is left. Remove buds and leaves from the lower 4 in, dip the heel in fertilizer, and plant the cutting firmly in a pot or trench. Keep well watered.

Softwood cuttings (carnations, geraniums, delphiniums, chrysanthemums, etc.) Take cuttings in the summer. Choose a young shoot up to 5 in long according to the size of the plant. Cut off below a leaf joint. Trim off lower leaves and buds to leave 3 to 5 pairs of leaves at the top. Dip the end in fertilizer and plant in a pot box. Softwood cuttings need a damp, close atmosphere.

How to Grow Plants in a Straight Row

To produce straight rows of plants in your garden, follow this easy method. Place the head of a garden rake along the edge of the plot so that the handle lies across the soil (a). Tread gently on the handle to make an indent (b). Remove the rake and sow seeds along the indent (c), and the plants will come up in neat parallel rows (d).

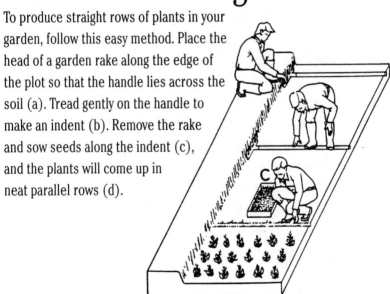

How to Keep Plants Happy

Plants, like humans beings, are sensitive to their environment and relate to the temperaments and moods of people. A hostile gardener who ignores his plants will induce wilting. A gardener who is violent in ripping them up will cause fear and shrinking; the picked plants will die sooner and those remaining in the soil will be traumatized and stunted. But a gardener who speaks encouragingly and soothingly to his plants, and who approaches them with real affection, will make them grow and flourish.

It may seem anthropomorphic to use the words like mood and emotion about plants, but the measurable electrostatic and chemical changes in plants are as real as those that occur in us when emotional changes take place. Plants, to some extent, are telepathic, and they will distinguish between gestures of hostility and those of nurturing. One of the ways to keep your plants happy is to talk to them in the same way you would a pet or a child, another way is to play pleasant music: Mozart or Bach or some gentle Schubert seem to have the best effects. Plants' nerves, like those of experimental rats and some human beings, can, it seems, be jangled by harsh pop music or a violent cocophany of sounds.

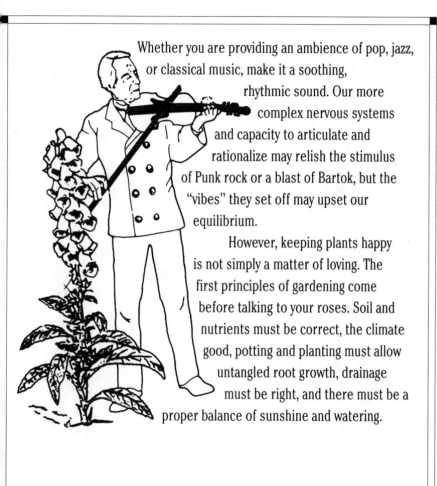

Whether you are providing an ambience of pop, jazz, or classical music, make it a soothing, rhythmic sound. Our more complex nervous systems and capacity to articulate and rationalize may relish the stimulus of Punk rock or a blast of Bartok, but the "vibes" they set off may upset our equilibrium.

However, keeping plants happy is not simply a matter of loving. The first principles of gardening come before talking to your roses. Soil and nutrients must be correct, the climate good, potting and planting must allow untangled root growth, drainage must be right, and there must be a proper balance of sunshine and watering.

How to Keep Birds at Bay

Birds can be a nuisance and a blessing. They can destroy buds and seedlings and damage fruit but many do eat insects that can attack your plants. An old-fashioned scarecrow will often keep them away. Commercial growers sometimes use scaring mechanisms that let off small controlled explosions at intervals. If you have a lot of fruit it may be worth investing in commercial fruit cages. To keep birds off seedlings, drive pegs at the end of rows and attach crisscrossed cotton thread to make it difficult for them to land.

Plastic bags tied to poles and strings off glinting foil will flap in the wind and help frighten the birds away. Change methods now and again so the birds do not get too used to them. For soft fruit, whether low-level strawberries or tall raspberries, use nylon netting stretched over them to give the best protection.

How to Preserve Leaves and Flowers

There are three ways to preserve plant material: drying them in air, with a desiccant (drying) powder, or with glycerin. Some plants are better suited to one method than another.

Air-drying Suitable for grasses, seedheads, everlasting flowers, and a few others such as acanthus, goldenrod, mimosa, and sea holly. Cut flowers on a warm, dry day, just before they are fully open. Remove leaves. Tie small flowers in bunches with a loop to hang them up. Hang larger flowers separately, or stand them upright in a jar. Average drying time: 1-3 weeks.

Desiccant powder Use, in order of preference, silica gel crystals, borax, sand. Put a layer of crystals or powder in the bottom of a box, lay the flowers on top, and cover with more powder. Average drying time: two days. You can dry and reuse the material. This method suits a wide variety of flowers.

Glycerin About the only method for leaves. Make a mixture of two parts of hot water to one of glycerin and stand the stems of your sprays of leaves in it. In 4-5 days the water in the leaves will be replaced by glycerin and they will have turned dark.

How to Make a Zen Garden

A Japanese sand garden – or zen garden – is sparse in design but rich in the contemplative space it offers the beholder. To sit and meditate upon it is to glimpse the layer structure of existence; the garden is a small sea, a wide ocean, cloudtops, a vast and undefined universe – or is it all of these things at the same time?

As a site for your garden, choose a small area relatively free from wind. Give the ground a slight slope to improve drainage. Pour in a concrete bed or cover with a sheet of vinyl and punch holes in it where water can seep out. Don't leave the earth bare; mud will come to the surface after a rain and spoil the garden's appearance. Spread crushed granite (not beach sand) over the bed to a depth of 2.5 to 3 inches.

Add a large rock grouping in one corner or scatter smaller groupings seemingly at random through the garden. Avoid symmetry and keep your design simple. Rake

in decorative wave or ripple patterns with a serrated piece of wood. Renew or change the pattern every week or so. Add moss or tiny plantings around the bases of the rocks to soften their lines. Coniferous trees (pines, junipers, etc.) planted on the border of the garden provide a good color counterpoint throughout the year and make the mood a little less austere. Try not to use deciduous trees as their leaves will fall out into the garden and crumble, and it will take hours to pick them out.

How to Make Perfumes

To make most perfumes you need a still, so that you can extract the essential oils from flowers and other scented raw materials. To make up perfume dissolve 10 parts of essential oils in 90 parts of pure alcohol; colognes consist of essential oils 3-5 percent, alcohol 80-90 percent, water to 100 percent; toilet waters contain 2 percent essential oils, 60-80 percent alcohol, the rest water. If you do not have a still, here's a simple recipe for lavender water:

Essence of musk	½ fl oz or 15 ml
Essence of ambergris	½ fl oz or 15 ml
Oil of cinnamon	10 drops
English lavender	¾ fl oz or 7.5 ml
Oil of geranium	¼ fl oz or 4 ml
Alcohol or wine	20 fl oz or 600 ml

Use either U.S. or metric measurements. Mix together well, and keep in a well-stoppered bottle. If you have a still, steep flower heads or other perfume ingredients, such as sandalwood, in spirits of wine for several weeks, then distill the infusion.

How to Identify a Diamond

Diamonds may be a girl's best friend but she'd better make sure they are real ones. There are two quick ways of checking. Breathe on it. If it clouds over, then it is almost certainly fake, for most imitation stones have lower specific heat. Then try dropping it into a glass of water. You may see a joint that was previously invisible. The refraction of the light in the water may suddenly reveal that the stone is actually two pieces stuck together; one form of saving money is to stick a real top on a cheap bottom.

Diamonds always have sharp corners and facets. The reflections and refractions in the stone are bright and confusing. Hold the stone at arm's length and look at it horizontally; now slowly tilt it. The refraction in the stone should be so strong that you cannot ever see through it. Don't try the old Kimberley test of hitting the stone with a hammer. If it damages the hammer you can be pretty sure you've got a diamond, but if the hammer shatters the stone, it doesn't necessarily mean it was fake!

How to Culture a Pearl

Take a healthy, live oyster, preferably one of the species belonging to the genus Pinctada, the small oysters used by the commercial pearl industry in Japan, and a tiny bead made from the shell of a freshwater bivalve. Enclose the bead in a small bag of tissue from the mantle of another oyster. Wedge open the living oyster and insert the bag into its reproductive area. Return the oyster to sheltered water in which phytoplanktonic food is abundant. If you wish, remove it after a few weeks to see whether the graft has survived (many do not). If it does, a pearl of nacre will be formed around the shell fragment, a process which may take several years. To keep the oysters readily accessible, commercial pearl farms keep them in baskets or cages slung beneath rafts. The pearl will be almost identical to the naturally produced article, the nature of the particle within it being the only difference.